best of the best
APPETIZERS

Publications International, Ltd.

Favorite Brand Name Recipes at www.fbnr.com

Pictured on the front cover: Maple-Glazed Meatballs *(page 38).*
Pictured on the back cover: Chipotle Chicken Quesadillas *(page 106).*

ISBN-13: 978-1-4127-1671-0
ISBN-10: 1-4127-1671-3

Library of Congress Control Number: 2008934197

Manufactured in China.

8 7 6 5 4 3 2 1

Microwave Cooking: Microwave ovens vary in wattage. Use the cooking times as guidelines and check for doneness before adding more time.

Preparation/Cooking Times: Preparation times are based on the approximate amount of time required to assemble the recipe before cooking, baking, chilling or serving. These times include preparation steps such as measuring, chopping and mixing. The fact that some preparations and cooking can be done simultaneously is taken into account. Preparation of optional ingredients and serving suggestions is not included.

contents

ultimate
dips & spreads

Sweet Fruit Dip

**4 ounces (½ of 8-ounce package) PHILADELPHIA®
Cream Cheese, softened**
1 cup whole berry cranberry sauce
1 cup thawed COOL WHIP® Whipped Topping

BEAT cream cheese and cranberry sauce with electric mixer on medium speed until well blended. Gently stir in whipped topping; cover.

REFRIGERATE at least 1 hour or until ready to serve.

SERVE with strawberries, red and green grapes, pineapple, kiwi or pears, cut into bite-size pieces for dipping.

Makes 16 servings, 2 tablespoons each

Fun Idea: This dip is great spooned over individual servings of cut-up fresh fruit.

Substitution: Prepare as directed, using **PHILADELPHIA®** Neufchâtel Cheese, ⅓ Less Fat than Cream Cheese and **COOL WHIP LITE®** Whipped Topping.

Prep Time: 10 minutes
Total Time: 1 hour 10 minutes

BLT Dip

1 envelope LIPTON® RECIPE SECRETS® Onion Soup Mix*
1 container (8 ounces) sour cream
1 cup HELLMANN'S® or BEST FOODS® Real Mayonnaise
1 medium tomato, chopped (about 1 cup)
½ cup cooked crumbled bacon (about 6 slices) or bacon bits
   Shredded lettuce

Also terrific with LIPTON® RECIPE SECRETS® Golden Onion Soup Mix.

1. In medium bowl, combine all ingredients except lettuce; chill, if desired.

2. Garnish with lettuce and serve with your favorite dippers.

Makes 3 cups dip

Prep Time: 10 minutes

Belgioioso® Gorgonzola Spread with Walnuts

12 walnut halves
 1 pound BELGIOIOSO® Mascarpone, at room temperature
 5 ounces BELGIOIOSO® Gorgonzola, at room temperature
 1 tablespoon cognac
 1 bunch fresh chives, finely chopped
   Salt and freshly ground pepper

Grate the walnuts; set aside. Combine the BELGIOIOSO® Mascarpone and BELGIOIOSO® Gorgonzola in a dish and mash them together with a fork, incorporating the cognac and a little salt and pepper. When the mixture is smooth, add the walnuts and chives. Mix again until well blended. Spoon into a serving bowl.

Makes 8 servings

Tip: Walnuts and Gorgonzola are a favorite European pairing. Serve with yogurt quick bread, toasted whole-grain country breads, or breadsticks.

BLT Dip

Robust Cheddar, Feta and Walnut Cheese Log

8 ounces (2 cups) grated California Cheddar cheese
8 ounces (1 cup) cream cheese
4 ounces (¾ cup) crumbled California feta cheese
2 cloves garlic, minced
¼ teaspoon salt
¼ teaspoon hot pepper sauce
1 cup chopped California walnuts, toasted if desired, divided
2 tablespoons capers, drained
2 tablespoons chopped, roasted and peeled red bell pepper *or* 2 tablespoons chopped pimientos
2 tablespoons gin or vodka (optional)
   Pinch cayenne pepper

Combine Cheddar cheese, cream cheese, feta cheese, garlic, salt and pepper sauce; mix until blended and smooth. Add ½ cup walnuts, capers, bell pepper and gin, if desired. Continue to mix until ingredients are incorporated and evenly blended. Mixture will be easier to shape if refrigerated 2 to 3 hours before forming.

Add cayenne pepper to remaining ½ cup walnuts and toss to coat. Spread nuts on sheet of waxed paper.

With damp hands, divide cheese mixture in half. Pat and press each half into ball about 3 inches across or into log about 5 inches long and 2 inches wide. (Shape does not need to be perfect.)

Roll each log or ball in walnuts, patting coating in firmly. Wrap in plastic wrap and chill until ready to serve.   *Makes 12 servings*

Feta and Fontina Walnut Cheese Ball: Omit the Cheddar and cream cheese and substitute 8 ounces (2 cups) grated California fontina cheese and 4 ounces (1 cup) grated California mozzarella cheese. Combine with the feta cheese and other ingredients as directed above. If desired, roll the balls or logs in a mixture of ¼ cup chopped parsley and ¼ cup dry bread crumbs or rye cracker crumbs.

Favorite recipe from **Walnut Marketing Board**

Robust Cheddar, Feta and Walnut Cheese Log

Santa Fe Pineapple Salsa

2 cups finely chopped fresh DOLE® Tropical Gold® Pineapple
1 can (8 ounces) red, pinto or kidney beans, rinsed and drained
1 can (8¼ ounces) whole kernel corn, drained
1 cup chopped green or red bell pepper
½ cup finely chopped DOLE® Red Onion
2 tablespoons chopped fresh cilantro
1 to 2 teaspoons seeded and chopped fresh jalapeño pepper
½ teaspoon grated lime peel
2 tablespoons lime juice

- Combine pineapple, beans, corn, bell pepper, onion, cilantro, jalapeño, lime peel and juice in medium serving bowl. Cover and chill at least 30 minutes to allow flavors to blend. Serve with grilled salmon and asparagus. Garnish with grilled pineapple wedges, if desired.

- Salsa can also be served as a dip with tortilla chips or spooned over quesadillas or tacos. *Makes 10 servings*

Prep Time: 20 minutes
Chill Time: 30 minutes

Southern Pimiento Cheese

1 package (3 ounces) cream cheese, softened
⅓ cup HELLMANN'S® or BEST FOODS® Real Mayonnaise
2 cups shredded Cheddar cheese (about 8 ounces)
½ cup drained and chopped pimientos (about 4 ounces)
½ cup finely chopped green onions
¼ cup finely chopped pimiento-stuffed green olives
1 teaspoon LAWRY'S® Garlic Powder with Parsley
1 teaspoon paprika

1. In medium bowl with wire whisk, beat cream cheese and Hellmann's or Best Foods Real Mayonnaise until smooth. Stir in remaining ingredients until blended. Chill until ready to serve.

2. Serve at room temperature and, if desired, with crackers or party-size bread. *Makes 2¼ cups spread*

Prep Time: 15 minutes
Chill Time: 30 minutes

Santa Fe Pineapple Salsa

Roasted Red Pepper Dip with Taco Chips

- 2 tablespoons olive oil
- 1 medium onion, chopped
- 3 tablespoons ORTEGA® Diced Green Chiles
- 2 teaspoons POLANER® Chopped Garlic
- 2 jars (12 ounces each) roasted red peppers, drained
- ½ cup ORTEGA® Thick & Chunky Salsa
- 2 tablespoons REGINA® Red Wine Vinegar
- 1 tablespoon packed brown sugar
- 1 teaspoon ground cumin
- ½ teaspoon salt
- 1 package (12-count) ORTEGA® Yellow Corn Taco Shells
  Additional salt, to taste

For Dip, heat oil in medium skillet. Add onion, chiles and garlic. Cook until onion begins to brown, about 4 minutes.

Place cooked onion mixture into food processor with red peppers, salsa, vinegar, brown sugar, cumin and salt. Process until mixture is puréed. Transfer to bowl and cover tightly. Chill at least 1 hour or up to 48 hours.

For Taco Chips, preheat oven to 350°F. Place taco shells on a baking sheet and bake 10 minutes. Remove from oven and gently break into pieces. Sprinkle with salt, if desired. Serve with dip.

Makes 2 cups dip

Prep Time: 10 minutes
Start to Finish: 30 minutes

Roasted Red Pepper Dip with Taco Chips

Cheesy Taco Dip

2 (15-ounce) cans black beans, drained
2 teaspoons vegetable oil
1 cup chopped onion
2 cloves garlic, minced
1 cup diced fresh tomato
1 cup mild picante or taco sauce
1 teaspoon ground cumin
1 teaspoon chili powder
2 tablespoons fresh lime juice
  Cooking spray
4 ounces grated CABOT® 50% Reduced Fat Jalapeno Cheddar or
  CABOT® 50% Reduced Fat Cheddar, divided
1 cup fat-free sour cream
½ cup chopped fresh cilantro
  Cherry tomatoes for garnish

1. Preheat oven to 350°F.

2. Place beans in large bowl; partially mash until chunky. Set aside.

3. In large skillet over medium heat, heat oil until hot. Add onion and garlic and cook, stirring constantly, until onion is tender. Add tomato, picante or taco sauce, cumin, chili powder and reserved beans; cook, stirring constantly, for 5 minutes. Remove from heat and stir in lime juice.

4. Coat 9-inch pie plate with cooking spray. Spread half of bean mixture in pie plate and sprinkle with half of cheese. Top with remaining bean mixture, spreading evenly to cover cheese. Cover with foil and bake for 20 minutes.

5. Uncover and let stand for 10 minutes. Spread sour cream evenly over bean mixture, then sprinkle with remaining cheese and cilantro. Garnish with cherry tomatoes. Serve warm with baked tortilla chips.

Makes about 32 servings

Middle Eastern Chick-Pea Dip (Hummus)

2 cans (15 ounces each) chick-peas, drained and rinsed
¼ cup tahini or peanut butter
¼ cup olive oil
¼ cup *Frank's® RedHot® Original Cayenne Pepper Sauce*
2 tablespoons fresh lemon juice
3 cloves garlic, chopped
½ teaspoon salt
Crackers or pita bread wedges
Vegetable dippers

1. Place chick-peas, *⅓ cup water,* tahini, olive oil, ***Frank's RedHot*** Sauce, lemon juice, garlic and salt in food processor. Cover; process until very smooth. Transfer to serving bowl. Cover; refrigerate 1 hour.

2. Let stand at room temperature 30 minutes before serving. Serve with crackers or pita bread wedges and vegetable dippers.

Makes 3 cups dip

Prep Time: 15 minutes
Chill Time: 1 hour

note

Hummus may be used as a sandwich spread. It's great with grilled vegetables such as eggplant, zucchini and red bell peppers.

Feta Cheese and Sun-Dried Tomato Spread

1 package (8 ounces) PHILADELPHIA® Cream Cheese, softened
1 package (4 ounces) ATHENOS® Traditional Crumbled Feta Cheese
2 tablespoons chopped fresh basil
2 tablespoons finely chopped sun-dried tomatoes

MIX all ingredients until well blended; cover.

REFRIGERATE several hours or until chilled.

SERVE as a spread on **NABISCO**® Crackers or fresh vegetables.

Makes 1½ cups

Prep Time: 10 minutes
Total Time: 3 hours 10 minutes

Philadelphia® Greek-Style Spread

1 package (8 ounces) PHILADELPHIA® Cream Cheese, softened
½ cup chopped tomato
¼ cup chopped pitted Niçoise olives
¼ cup finely chopped cucumber
1 teaspoon olive oil
½ teaspoon dried oregano leaves, crushed

SPREAD cream cheese on serving plate.

MIX remaining ingredients; spoon over cream cheese.

SERVE with assorted **NABISCO**® Crackers or toasted pita wedges.

Makes 10 servings, 2 tablespoons each

Prep Time: 10 minutes

Feta Cheese and Sun-Dried Tomato Spread

Olive Tapenade Dip

1½ cups (10-ounce jar) pitted kalamata olives, drained
3 tablespoons olive oil
3 tablespoons *French's®* Spicy Brown Mustard
1 tablespoon minced fresh rosemary leaves *or*
    1 teaspoon dried rosemary leaves
1 teaspoon minced garlic

1. Place all ingredients in food processor. Process until puréed.

2. Serve with vegetable crudités or pita chips.

Makes 4 (¼-cup) servings

Tip: To pit olives, place in plastic bag. Gently tap with wooden mallet or rolling pin until olives split open. Remove pits.

Hot Cheesy Spinach & Artichoke Dip

1 package (10 ounces) frozen chopped spinach, thawed and
    squeezed dry
1 package (8 ounces) cream cheese, softened
¾ cup HELLMANN'S® or BEST FOODS® Real Mayonnaise
1½ cups shredded cheddar or Monterey Jack cheese (about 6 ounces)
1 package KNORR® Vegetable Recipe Mix
1 can (14 ounces) artichoke hearts, drained and chopped
1 can (8 ounces) water chestnuts, drained and chopped
2 cloves garlic, finely chopped

1. Preheat oven to 350°F.

2. In medium bowl, combine all ingredients except ½ cup cheddar cheese. Spoon into 2-quart casserole, then top with remaining ½ cup cheddar cheese.

3. Bake 35 minutes or until heated through. Serve, if desired, with toasted French baguette rounds, sliced garlic bread, corn or tortilla chips or vegetable dippers.

Makes about 4 cups dip

Spanakopita Dip: Substitute feta cheese for the cheddar and eliminate the artichoke hearts. Spoon into mini phyllo cups and bake 8 minutes or until filling puffs.

Olive Tapenade Dip

Garden Vegetable Dip

2 packages (8 ounces each) PHILADELPHIA® Cream Cheese, softened
½ cup KRAFT® Blue Cheese Dressing
½ cup finely chopped broccoli
1 medium carrot, shredded

MIX cream cheese and dressing until well blended. Stir in vegetables; cover.

REFRIGERATE several hours or until chilled.

SERVE with assorted **NABISCO®** Crackers.

Makes 20 servings, 2 tablespoons each

Best of Season: Take advantage of the fresh seasonal vegetables that are available. Cut up zucchini, cucumbers and bell peppers to serve as dippers with this creamy dip.

Variation: Prepare as directed, using **PHILADELPHIA®** Neufchâtel Cheese, ⅓ Less Fat than Cream Cheese and **KRAFT®** Light Blue Cheese Reduced Fat Dressing.

Prep Time: 10 minutes
Total Time: 3 hours 10 minutes

Zesty Liver Pâté

⅓ cup butter or margarine
1 pound chicken livers
¾ cup coarsely chopped green onions
¾ cup chopped fresh parsley
½ cup dry white wine
¾ teaspoon Original TABASCO® brand Pepper Sauce
½ teaspoon salt
Crackers or French bread

Melt butter in large saucepan; add chicken livers, onions and parsley. Sauté until livers are evenly browned and cooked through. Transfer to blender or food processor container. Add wine, TABASCO® Sauce and salt; cover. Process until smooth. Pour into decorative crock-style jar with lid. Chill until thick enough to spread. Serve with crackers or French bread.   *Makes about 2 cups pâté*

Garden Vegetable Dip

Quick Cheesy Fondue

1 can (10½ ounces) CAMPBELL'S® Condensed French Onion Soup
¼ cup dry sherry
1 package (8 ounces) cream cheese, softened
1 cup shredded Gruyére cheese (4 ounces)

Suggested Dippers

French bread cubes, warm PEPPERIDGE FARM® Garlic Bread, cut
into cubes, cooked meatballs, cubes of deli roast beef, steamed
baby red potatoes

MIX soup and sherry in medium saucepan over medium heat for
5 minutes for alcohol to evaporate. Add cream cheese. Heat
through, stirring occasionally. Add Gruyére cheese. Cook until
cheeses are melted.

POUR into a fondue pot or slow cooker. Serve warm with dippers.

Makes 2½ cups

Prep Time: 5 minutes
Cook Time: 10 minutes

To soften cream cheese, remove from wrapper.
On microwavable plate, microwave on HIGH 15 seconds.

Quick Cheesy Fondue

crowd-pleasing snacks

One-Bite Burgers

1 package (11 ounces) refrigerated breadstick dough
   (12 breadsticks)
1 pound ground beef
2 teaspoons garlic or lemon pepper seasoning
9 slices Cheddar or American cheese, quartered (optional)
36 round dill pickle slices
   Ketchup or mustard

1. Preheat oven to 375°F. Separate dough into 12 breadsticks; cut each breadstick into 3 equal pieces. Working with one piece at a time, tuck ends under to meet at center, pressing to seal and form very small bun about 1½ inches in diameter and ½ inch high.

2. Place buns seam side down on ungreased baking sheet. Bake 11 to 14 minutes or until golden brown. Remove to wire racks.

3. Meanwhile, gently mix ground beef and seasoning in large bowl. Shape beef mixture into 36 patties, using about 2 teaspoons beef per patty.

4. Heat large skillet over medium heat. Cook patties 7 to 8 minutes or until patties are cooked through, turning once. Top with cheese slice, if desired.

5. Split buns in half crosswise. Place burgers on bottom bun halves. Top with pickle slices, small dollops of ketchup or mustard and bun tops.   *Makes 36 mini burgers*

Three Pepper Quesadillas

1 cup *each* thin green, red and yellow bell pepper strips
½ cup thin onion slices
⅓ cup butter *or* margarine
½ teaspoon ground cumin
1 package (8 ounces) PHILADELPHIA® Cream Cheese, softened
1 package (8 ounces) KRAFT® Shredded Sharp Cheddar Cheese
10 TACO BELL® HOME ORIGINALS®* Flour Tortillas
1 jar (16 ounces) TACO BELL® HOME ORIGINALS®* Thick 'N Chunky Salsa

TACO BELL and HOME ORIGINALS are registered trademarks owned and licensed by Taco Bell Corp.

PREHEAT oven to 425°F. Cook and stir peppers and onion in butter in large skillet on medium-high heat until crisp-tender. Stir in cumin. Drain, reserving liquid.

BEAT cream cheese and Cheddar cheese with electric mixer on medium speed until well blended. Spoon 2 tablespoons cheese mixture onto each tortilla; top each evenly with pepper mixture. Fold tortillas in half; place on ungreased baking sheet. Brush with reserved liquid.

BAKE 10 minutes or until heated through. Cut each tortilla into thirds. Serve warm with salsa. *Makes 30 servings, 1 piece each*

Make Ahead: Prepare as directed except for baking; cover. Refrigerate. When ready to serve, bake, uncovered, at 425°F, 15 to 18 minutes or until thoroughly heated through.

Prep Time: 20 minutes
Bake Time: 10 minutes

Three Pepper Quesadillas

Cheesy Chicken Nachos

   2 tablespoons olive oil
   1 onion, diced
   1 teaspoon POLANER® Chopped Garlic
   1 pound ground chicken
   1 jar (16 ounces) ORTEGA® Salsa, any variety, divided
   2 teaspoons dried parsley
   1 teaspoon ORTEGA® Chili Seasoning Mix
   1 teaspoon REGINA® Red Wine Vinegar
  ½ cup water
 12 ORTEGA® Yellow Corn Taco Shells, broken
   1 pound shredded taco cheese blend (4 cups)
   1 can (15 ounces) JOAN OF ARC® Black Beans
   1 jar (12 ounces) ORTEGA® Sliced Jalapeños

Heat oil in skillet over medium-high heat until hot. Add onion and garlic. Cook and stir until onions are translucent, about 3 minutes. Stir in chicken, ¾ cup salsa, parsley, seasoning mix, vinegar and ½ cup water; cook until meat is cooked through and sauce begins to thicken, about 5 minutes.

Preheat broiler; place rack about 7 inches from top of oven.

Assemble nachos by arranging broken taco shells on baking sheet. Sprinkle on 2 cups cheese; top with chicken mixture, black beans and jalapeños. Add remaining salsa and cheese. (If desired, prepare individual portions by dividing recipe among 6 heat-resistant plates.)

Place under broiler 4 minutes or until cheese begins to melt.

Makes 6 servings

Note: Be sure to have some of your favorite guacamole, sour cream and black olives on hand to place on top of the nachos.

Variation: If you have ground beef on hand, you can still make these tasty nachos. Just brown the meat first and discard the excess fat before proceeding as directed. Or try this recipe with ground turkey.

Prep Time: 10 minutes
Start to Finish: 20 minutes

Cheesy Chicken Nachos

Original Buffalo Chicken Wings

Zesty Blue Cheese Dip (page 32)
2½ pounds chicken wings, split and tips discarded
½ cup *Frank's® RedHot®* Original Cayenne Pepper Sauce (or to taste)
⅓ cup butter or margarine, melted
Celery sticks

1. Prepare Zesty Blue Cheese Dip.

2. Deep fry* wings at 400°F 12 minutes or until crisp and no longer pink; drain.

3. Combine ***Frank's RedHot*** Sauce and butter in large bowl. Add wings to sauce; toss well to coat evenly. Serve with Zesty Blue Cheese Dip and celery.   *Makes 24 to 30 individual pieces*

*Or, prepare wings using one of the cooking methods below. Add wings to sauce; toss well to coat evenly.

To Bake: Place wings in single layer on rack in foil-lined roasting pan. Bake at 425°F 1 hour or until crisp and no longer pink, turning once halfway through baking time.

To Broil: Place wings in single layer on rack in foil-lined roasting pan. Broil 6 inches from heat 15 to 20 minutes or until crisp and no longer pink, turning once halfway through cooking time.

To Grill: Place wings on oiled grid. Grill over medium heat 30 to 40 minutes or until crisp and no longer pink, turning often.

Prep Time: 10 minutes
Cook Time: 15 minutes

continued on page 32

Original Buffalo Chicken Wings

Original Buffalo Chicken Wings, continued

Shanghai Red Wings: Cook chicken wings as directed on page 30. Combine ¼ cup soy sauce, 3 tablespoons honey, 3 tablespoons **Frank's RedHot** Sauce, 2 tablespoons peanut oil, 1 teaspoon grated peeled fresh ginger and 1 teaspoon minced garlic in small bowl. Mix well. Pour sauce over wings; toss well to coat evenly.

Cajun Wings: Cook chicken wings as directed on page 30. Combine ⅓ cup **Frank's RedHot** Sauce, ⅓ cup ketchup, ¼ cup (½ stick) melted butter or margarine and 2 teaspoons Cajun seasoning in small bowl. Mix well. Pour sauce over wings; toss well to coat evenly.

Santa Fe Wings: Cook chicken wings as directed on page 30. Combine ¼ cup (½ stick) melted butter or margarine, ¼ cup **Frank's RedHot** Sauce, ¼ cup chili sauce and 1 teaspoon chili powder in small bowl. Mix well. Pour sauce over wings; toss well to coat evenly.

Sweet 'n' Spicy Wings: Cook chicken wings as directed on page 30. Combine ⅓ cup **Frank's RedHot** Sauce, ¼ cup (½ stick) butter, 2 tablespoons each thawed frozen orange juice concentrate and honey, and ¼ teaspoon each ground cinnamon and ground allspice in small microwavable bowl. Microwave on HIGH 1 minute or until butter is melted. Stir until smooth. Pour sauce over wings; toss well to coat evenly.

Kentucky Style Wings: Cook chicken wings as directed on page 30. Combine ¼ cup (½ stick) melted butter or margarine, ¼ cup **Frank's RedHot** Sauce, 2 tablespoons pancake syrup and 2 tablespoons bourbon in large bowl. Mix well. Pour sauce over wings; toss well to coat evenly.

Zesty Blue Cheese Dip

½ cup blue cheese salad dressing
¼ cup sour cream
2 teaspoons *Frank's® RedHot®* Original Cayenne Pepper Sauce

Combine all ingredients in medium serving bowl; mix well. Garnish with crumbled blue cheese, if desired.   *Makes ¾ cup dip*

Prep Time: 5 minutes

Franks Under Wraps

½ of a 17.3-ounce package PEPPERIDGE FARM® Frozen Puff Pastry Sheets (1 sheet)
1 egg
1 tablespoon water
10 frankfurters (about 1 pound), cut crosswise into halves
Prepared mustard

1. Thaw the pastry sheet at room temperature for 40 minutes or until it's easy to handle. Heat the oven to 400°F. Lightly grease a baking sheet. Stir the egg and water in a small bowl.

2. Unfold the pastry on a lightly floured surface. Cut into 20 (½-inch) strips. Wrap the pastry strips around frankfurters, pressing gently to seal. Place 2 inches apart on the prepared baking sheet. Brush with the egg mixture.

3. Bake for 15 minutes or until golden. Serve with mustard for dipping. *Makes 20 appetizers*

For a Holiday Twist: Use 5 frankfurters and cut each into quarters lengthwise, then cut in half crosswise. Twist pastry strips while wrapping around 2 frankfurter pieces. Press gently to seal.

Thaw Time: 40 minutes
Prep Time: 15 minutes
Bake Time: 15 minutes

Bacon Appetizer Crescents

1 package (8 ounces) PHILADELPHIA® Cream Cheese, softened
8 slices OSCAR MAYER® Bacon, crisply cooked, crumbled
⅓ cup KRAFT® 100% Grated Parmesan Cheese
¼ cup finely chopped onion
2 tablespoons chopped fresh parsley
1 tablespoon milk
2 cans (8 ounces each) refrigerated crescent dinner rolls

PREHEAT oven to 375°F. Mix cream cheese, bacon, Parmesan cheese, onion, parsley and milk until well blended; set aside.

SEPARATE each can of dough into 8 triangles. Spread each triangle with 1 rounded tablespoonful of cream cheese mixture. Cut each triangle lengthwise into 3 narrow triangles. Roll up, starting at wide ends. Place point-side down on greased baking sheet.

BAKE 12 to 15 minutes or until golden brown. Serve warm.

Makes 4 dozen or 24 servings, 2 crescents each

Jazz It Up: Sprinkle lightly with poppy seeds before baking.

Prep Time: 30 minutes
Bake Time: 15 minutes

Ham and Cherry Roll-Ups

1 package (8 ounces) cream cheese, softened
½ cup sliced green onions
½ cup toasted chopped walnuts
¼ cup cherry preserves
1 pound sliced deli ham (16 to 20 slices)

In small bowl, stir together all ingredients except ham. Spread a rounded tablespoon of the cream cheese mixture on each ham slice. Roll up; cut each roll in half. Secure rolls with wooden picks. Refrigerate, covered, until serving time.

Makes 32 to 40 appetizers

Tip: Prepare and refrigerate these easy appetizers up to 1 day ahead.

Favorite recipe from **National Pork Board**

Bacon Appetizer Crescents

Touchdown Twists

½ of a 17.3-ounce package PEPPERIDGE FARM® Frozen
Puff Pastry Sheets (1 sheet)
¾ cup shredded Cheddar cheese
1 tablespoon butter, melted
¼ cup grated Parmesan cheese
¼ teaspoon ground black pepper

1. Thaw the pastry sheet at room temperature for 40 minutes or until it's easy to handle. Heat the oven to 400°F. Lightly grease a baking sheet.

2. Unfold the pastry sheet on a lightly floured surface. Roll the sheet into a 14×10-inch rectangle. Cut the pastry in half lengthwise. Top 1 rectangle with the Cheddar cheese. Place the remaining rectangle over the cheese-topped rectangle. Roll gently with a rolling pin to seal.

3. Cut crosswise into 28 (½-inch) strips. Brush the strips with melted butter then sprinkle with the Parmesan cheese and black pepper. Twist the strips and place 2 inches apart on the baking sheet, pressing down ends.

4. Bake for 10 minutes or until golden. Serve the twists warm or at room temperature. *Makes 28 twists*

Prep Time: 20 minutes
Thaw Time: 40 minutes
Bake Time: 10 minutes

Touchdown Twists

Maple-Glazed Meatballs

- 1½ cups ketchup
- 1 cup maple syrup or maple-flavored syrup
- ⅓ cup reduced-sodium soy sauce
- 1 tablespoon quick-cooking tapioca
- 1½ teaspoons ground allspice
- 1 teaspoon dry mustard
- 2 packages (about 16 ounces each) frozen fully cooked meatballs, partially thawed and separated
- 1 can (20 ounces) pineapple chunks in juice, drained

Slow Cooker Directions

1. Combine ketchup, maple syrup, soy sauce, tapioca, allspice and mustard in slow cooker.

2. Carefully stir meatballs and pineapple chunks into ketchup mixture.

3. Cover; cook on LOW 5 to 6 hours. Stir before serving.

Makes about 48 meatballs

Prep Time: 10 minutes
Cook Time: 5 to 6 hours

note

A slow cooker is a very useful appliance for entertaining, especially when preparing appetizers for a crowd. To save time, prepare one recipe early in the day; then simply walk away and return to the finished dish just before the party. Even better, using a slow cooker frees up your oven for other recipes. And, best of all, the slow cooker keeps hot foods warm for serving.

Chicken and Blue Cheese on Pumpernickel

½ **(16-ounce) package PERDUE® Fit 'N Easy® Thin-Sliced Skinless & Boneless Chicken Breast or Turkey Breast Cutlets**
⅓ **cup crumbled blue cheese**
¾ **tablespoon Dijon mustard**
   Salt and pepper, to taste
16 **slices cocktail pumpernickel, toasted and buttered**
½ **small red onion, very thinly sliced**
 1 **cup arugula, radicchio or watercress, very thinly sliced**

Set a large, non-stick skillet over high heat and coat it with cooking spray. Sauté chicken until golden brown on both sides and cooked through. Set aside to cool.

In a medium bowl, stir together blue cheese and mustard. Dice chicken and stir it in. Season to taste with salt and pepper.

To assemble, top each slice of bread with some onion, a heaping tablespoon of chicken and sprinkle with arugula. Serve immediately.

Makes 16 appetizers

Picante Chicken Quesadillas

 1 **can (10¾ ounces) CAMPBELL'S® Cheddar Cheese Soup**
1½ **cups chopped cooked chicken**
 ¼ **cup PACE® Picante Sauce**
 8 **flour tortillas (8 inches)**

1. Preheat the oven to 425°F.

2. Mix the soup, chicken and picante sauce.

3. Place the tortillas on 2 baking sheets. Top **half** of each tortilla with ¼ **cup** soup mixture. Spread to within ½ inch of edge. Moisten edges of tortilla with water. Fold over and press edges together.

4. Bake 5 minutes or until hot. *Makes 4 servings*

Prep Time: 10 minutes
Cook Time: 5 minutes

Beer-Battered Mushrooms

1 cup all-purpose flour
½ teaspoon baking powder
½ teaspoon chili powder
¼ teaspoon salt
⅛ teaspoon black pepper
1 cup beer
1 egg, separated
1 pound small mushrooms
1½ quarts vegetable oil
   Salt

1. Mix flour, baking powder, chili powder, salt and black pepper in medium bowl. Whisk together beer and egg yolk in small bowl. Wipe mushrooms clean with damp cloth or paper towel.

2. Beat egg whites in large bowl with electric mixer at medium speed until soft peaks form. Heat oil in 4-quart saucepan to 365°F.

3. Stir beer mixture into flour mixture just until blended. Fold in egg whites.

4. Dip mushrooms, 4 to 5 at a time, into batter and place carefully in hot oil. Fry mushrooms in batches, turning with tongs or slotted spoon until all sides are golden brown. Remove mushrooms to paper towels to drain. Sprinkle immediately with salt. (Do not allow oil temperature to dip below 365°F or rise above 375°F.) Stir batter between batches. Serve hot. *Makes 6 to 8 servings*

Beer-Battered Mushrooms

Hotsy Totsy Spiced Nuts

        1 can (12 ounces) mixed nuts
        3 tablespoons *Frank's® RedHot®* Original Cayenne Pepper Sauce
        1 tablespoon vegetable oil
        ¾ teaspoon seasoned salt
        ¾ teaspoon garlic powder

1. Preheat oven to 250°F. Place nuts in 15×10-inch jelly-roll pan. Combine remaining ingredients in small bowl; pour over nuts. Toss to coat evenly.

2. Bake 45 minutes or until nuts are toasted and dry, stirring every 15 minutes. Cool completely.   *Makes about 2 cups mix*

Prep Time: 5 minutes
Cook Time: 45 minutes

Mini Pizza Appetizers

        16 (½-inch-thick) slices French baguette, toasted
         1 cup quartered grape or cherry tomatoes
        ½ cup shredded mozzarella cheese (about 2 ounces)
        ¼ cup chopped pepperoni
        ¼ cup chopped red onion
        ¼ cup chopped pitted ripe olives
        40 sprays WISH-BONE® SALAD SPRITZERS® BALSAMIC BREEZE®
            Vinaigrette Dressing

1. Preheat oven to 400°F.

2. On baking sheet, arrange bread.

3. In medium bowl, combine remaining ingredients; evenly spoon on bread. Bake 10 minutes or until heated through and cheese is melted. Serve immediately.   *Makes 16 servings*

Prep Time: 20 minutes
Cook Time: 10 minutes

Top to bottom: Hotsy Totsy Spiced Nuts and
Zesty Party Snack Mix *(page 44)*

Zesty Party Snack Mix

4 cups oven-toasted corn cereal squares
2 cups *French's*® Potato Sticks
1 cup honey-roasted peanuts
3 tablespoons melted butter or vegetable oil
2 tablespoons *French's*® Worcestershire Sauce
2 tablespoons *Frank's*® *RedHot*® Original Cayenne Pepper Sauce
½ teaspoon seasoned salt

1. Place cereal, potato sticks and peanuts in 3-quart microwavable bowl. Combine melted butter, Worcestershire, **Frank's RedHot** Sauce and seasoned salt in small bowl; mix well. Pour butter mixture over cereal mixture. Toss to coat evenly.

2. Microwave, uncovered, on HIGH 6 minutes, stirring well every 2 minutes. Transfer to paper towels; cool completely.

Makes about 6 cups

Tex-Mex Snack Mix: Add 1 teaspoon each chili powder and ground cumin to butter mixture. Substitute 1 cup regular peanuts for honey-roasted nuts. Prepare as directed.

Italian Snack Mix: Add 1½ teaspoons Italian seasoning and ½ teaspoon garlic powder to butter mixture. Substitute ½ cup grated Parmesan cheese and ½ cup sliced almonds for honey-roasted nuts. Prepare as directed.

Indian Snack Mix: Omit seasoned salt. Add 2 teaspoons each sesame seeds and curry powder and ¼ teaspoon garlic salt to butter mixture. Substitute 1 cup cashews for honey-roasted nuts. Prepare as directed.

Prep Time: 10 minutes
Cook Time: 6 minutes

Party Meatballs

1½ pounds ground beef
⅓ cup dry bread crumbs
1 egg, beaten
⅓ cup finely chopped onion
1 can (10¾ ounces) CAMPBELL'S® Condensed Golden
   Mushroom Soup
½ cup sour cream
¼ cup water
2 teaspoons Worcestershire sauce
Chopped fresh parsley

1. Thoroughly mix the beef, bread crumbs, egg and onion in a large bowl. Shape the mixture firmly into 60 (1-inch) meatballs. Place the meatballs on a 15×10-inch baking pan.

2. Heat the broiler. Broil the meatballs with the top of the meatballs 4 inches from the heat for 5 minutes or until browned, turning halfway during cooking. Spoon off any fat.

3. Heat the soup, sour cream, water and Worcestershire in a 12-inch skillet over low heat.

4. Add the meatballs to the skillet. Cook and stir for 10 minutes or until hot and meatballs are cooked through. Do not let the mixture boil. Sprinkle with the parsley.   *Makes 60 appetizers*

Prep Time: 10 minutes
Broil Time: 5 minutes
Cook Time: 15 minutes

Ortega® Hot Poppers

1 can (3½ ounces) ORTEGA® Whole Jalapeños, drained
1 cup (4 ounces) shredded Cheddar cheese
1 package (3 ounces) cream cheese, softened
¼ cup chopped fresh cilantro
½ cup all-purpose flour
2 eggs, lightly beaten
2 cups cornflake cereal, crushed
   Vegetable oil
   ORTEGA® Salsa, any variety
   Sour cream

CUT jalapeños lengthwise into halves; remove seeds.

BLEND Cheddar cheese, cream cheese and cilantro in small bowl. Place 1 to 1½ teaspoons cheese mixture into each jalapeño half; chill for 15 minutes or until cheese is firm.

DIP each jalapeño half in flour; shake off excess. Dip in eggs; coat with cornflake crumbs.

ADD vegetable oil to 1-inch depth in medium skillet; heat over high heat for 1 minute. Fry jalapeños turning frequently with tongs, until golden brown on all sides. Remove from skillet; drain on paper towels. Serve with salsa and sour cream. *Makes 8 servings*

note

Whether you're hosting a party to watch your favorite team or planning a weekend gathering, serve hot poppers. Your guests will be thrilled to find that these taste just like those served in the local pub!

Ortega® Hot Poppers

Tex-Mex Potato Skins

 3 hot baked potatoes, split lengthwise
 ¾ cup (3 ounces) shredded Cheddar or pepper Jack cheese
1⅓ cups *French's®* French Fried Onions, divided
 ¼ cup chopped green chilies
 ¼ cup crumbled cooked bacon
   Salsa and sour cream

1. Preheat oven to 350°F. Scoop out inside of potatoes, leaving ¼-inch shells. Reserve inside of potatoes for another use.

2. Arrange potato halves on baking sheet. Top with cheese, ⅔ cup French Fried Onions, chilies and bacon.

3. Bake 15 minutes or until heated through and cheese is melted. Cut each potato half crosswise into thirds. Serve topped with salsa, sour cream and remaining onions.   *Makes 18 appetizer servings*

Tip: To bake potatoes quickly, microwave at HIGH 10 to 12 minutes or until tender.

Variation: For added Cheddar flavor, substitute *French's ®* **Cheddar French Fried Onions** for the original flavor.

Prep Time: 15 minutes
Cook Time: 15 minutes

Cocktail Bites

1¼ cups red currant jelly or cranberry sauce
1¼ cups ketchup
 2 pounds HILLSHIRE FARM® Lit'l Smokies

Heat jelly and ketchup in small saucepan over medium heat *or* microwave, uncovered, at HIGH 1 to 2 minutes or until mixture blends smoothly. Add Lit'l Smokies; cook until links are hot. Serve with frilled toothpicks.   *Makes about 100 hors d'oeuvres*

Tex-Mex Potato Skins

Bacon and Chipotle Cheddar Canapes

5 slices bacon, finely chopped and cooked
2 tablespoons onion, finely chopped
2 teaspoons drained prepared horseradish
¼ teaspoon salt
⅛ teaspoon black pepper
6 very thin slices firm white sandwich bread
6 slices SARGENTO® Deli Style Sliced Chipotle Cheddar Cheese

1. Stir together bacon, onion, horseradish, salt and pepper in a bowl with a rubber spatula until well blended.

2. Spread about 1½ tablespoons mixture evenly to edges of each slice of bread. Top with sliced cheese.

3. Cut each slice of bread into 4 squares or triangles. Bake on baking sheet about 10 minutes, until cheese is melted and beginning to brown on edges. Serve immediately.

Makes 24 appetizers

Tip: Assemble ahead of time. Cover and freeze. Bake about 20 minutes, until cheese is melted and beginning to brown on the edges.

Bake Time: 10 minutes

Mini Sausage Quiches

½ cup butter or margarine, softened
3 ounces cream cheese, softened
1 cup all-purpose flour
½ pound BOB EVANS® Italian Roll Sausage
1 cup (4 ounces) shredded Swiss cheese
1 tablespoon snipped fresh chives
2 eggs
1 cup half-and-half
¼ teaspoon salt
   Dash cayenne pepper

Beat butter and cream cheese in medium bowl until creamy. Blend in flour; refrigerate 1 hour. Roll into 24 (1-inch) balls; press each into ungreased mini muffin cup to form pastry shell. Preheat oven to 375°F. To prepare filling, crumble sausage into small skillet. Cook over medium heat until browned, stirring occasionally. Drain off any drippings. Sprinkle evenly into pastry shells in muffin cups; sprinkle with Swiss cheese and chives. Whisk eggs, half-and-half, salt and cayenne until blended; pour into pastry shells. Bake 20 to 30 minutes or until set. Remove from pans. Serve hot. Refrigerate leftovers.

Makes 24 appetizers

note

Individual quiches are a popular party finger food. To make the preparation more convenient, prepare the dough for the crust ahead of time and refrigerate for up to 1 day.

Deviled Ham Finger Sandwiches

1 package (8 ounces) PHILADELPHIA® Cream Cheese, softened
1 can (4.25 ounces) deviled ham
¼ cup KRAFT® Mayo Real Mayonnaise
10 small stuffed green olives, finely chopped
36 slices white bread, crusts removed

MIX cream cheese, ham, mayo and olives until well blended.

SPREAD each of 18 of the bread slices with about 2 tablespoons of the cream cheese mixture. Cover with remaining bread slices to make 18 sandwiches.

CUT each sandwich into quarters.

Makes 18 servings, 4 sandwich quarters each

Make Ahead: Prepare cream cheese mixture as directed. Cover and refrigerate up to 5 days. Spread onto bread slices and continue as directed. For easier spreading, mix 1 tablespoon milk with chilled cream cheese mixture before spreading onto bread slices. Or prepare sandwiches as directed, but do not cut into quarters. Wrap in plastic wrap. Refrigerate until ready to serve. Cut into quarters just before serving.

Substitution: Substitute **MIRACLE WHIP®** Dressing for the mayo.

Prep Time: 15 minutes

Deviled Ham Finger Sandwiches

dazzling party noshes

Pumpkin Ravioli

½ **cup solid-pack pumpkin**
¼ **teaspoon salt**
¼ **teaspoon black pepper**
 1 **package (14 ounces) wonton wrappers**
   Whole flat-leaf parsley leaves
 2 **tablespoons extra-virgin olive oil**
 2 **tablespoons butter**
 2 **to 3 cloves garlic, minced**
 2 **tablespoons chopped walnuts**
¾ **cup shredded Parmesan cheese**

1. Combine pumpkin, salt and pepper in medium bowl; taste and adjust seasonings. Place small bowl of water on work surface.

2. Unwrap wontons; cover with plastic wrap. Place 4 wontons in line on work surface. Brush 2 wontons with water, then place parsley leaf on each wet surface. Top each leaf with another wonton, pressing out air and sealing edges. Brush 1 layered wonton with water, then place 1 teaspoon pumpkin mixture in center of wonton. Top with remaining layered wonton, pressing out air and sealing all edges. Using 3-inch round or star cookie cutter, cut ravioli to shape, discarding trimmings. Repeat with remaining wontons, parsley leaves and pumpkin filling. Keep finished ravioli covered with plastic wrap until ready to cook.

continued on page 56

Pumpkin Ravioli, continued

3. Heat oil in large skillet over medium-low heat. Add butter and garlic. Cook 1 minute or until garlic is fragrant. Reduce heat to low.

4. Bring large pot of salted water to a boil. In small batches, slip ravioli into water. Cook 1 minute or until they float to the surface. Remove; drain well.

5. Transfer to skillet; coat with oil-butter mixture. Cook 1 to 2 minutes or until heated through; sprinkle with walnuts and cheese.

Makes 4 servings

Festive Crab Toasts

12 ounces crabmeat, flaked
1 can (10¾ ounces) condensed cream of celery soup, undiluted
¼ cup chopped celery
¼ cup sliced green onions
1 tablespoon lemon juice
⅛ teaspoon grated lemon peel
1 (8-ounce) French bread baguette
⅓ cup grated Parmesan cheese
Paprika

1. Combine crabmeat, soup, celery, green onions, lemon juice and lemon peel in medium bowl; mix well. Cut baguette diagonally into ½-inch slices; arrange slices on 2 ungreased baking sheets. Broil 5 inches from heat 2 minutes or until toasted, turning once.

2. Spread 1 tablespoon crab mixture onto each baguette slice. Sprinkle with Parmesan cheese and paprika. Broil 5 inches from heat 2 minutes or until lightly browned. *Makes about 30 toasts*

Festive Crab Toasts

Honey Holiday Wraps

- 1 box frozen puff pastry sheets, thawed according to package directions
- 1 egg, beaten
- ¼ cup Honey Mustard Sauce (recipe follows)
- ½ pound JENNIE-O TURKEY STORE® Deli Homestyle Honey Cured Turkey Breast, thinly sliced and finely diced
- ¼ cup walnuts, toasted and chopped
- 4 ounces Brie cheese, cut into 18 pieces

Preheat oven to 375°F. Remove pastry sheets from box and cut each into 9 smaller squares. Brush squares with egg and drizzle each with small amount of Honey Mustard Sauce. Toss diced JENNIE-O TURKEY STORE® Homestyle Honey Cured Turkey Breast with walnuts and then put about 1 teaspoon turkey mixture in center of each pastry square. Top with piece of Brie cheese; fold pastry over diagonally to form triangle, pressing edges to seal. Pinch together two corners on folded edge of pastry, and place tortellini shape on baking sheet. Bake at 375°F for 15 to 18 minutes. Allow to cool slightly before serving. Serve with additional Honey Mustard Sauce, if desired.

Makes 18 wraps

Honey Mustard Sauce: Mix together 2 tablespoons Dijon mustard and 2 tablespoons honey. Makes ¼ cup.

Variations: Any variety of JENNIE-O TURKEY STORE® turkey or chicken breast can be used in this recipe. Try apple butter or pesto sauce instead of honey mustard.

Prep Time: 30 minutes
Cook Time: 15 to 18 minutes

Honey Holiday Wraps

Stuffed Mushroom Caps

2 packages (8 ounces each) whole mushrooms
1 tablespoon butter
⅔ cup finely chopped cooked chicken
¼ cup grated Parmesan cheese
1 tablespoon chopped fresh basil
2 teaspoons lemon juice
⅛ teaspoon onion powder
⅛ teaspoon salt
  Pinch garlic powder
  Pinch black pepper
1 small package (3 ounces) cream cheese, softened
  Paprika

1. Preheat oven to 350°F. Remove stems from mushrooms and finely chop. Arrange mushroom caps, smooth side down, on greased baking sheet.

2. Melt butter in medium skillet over medium-high heat; cook chopped mushrooms 5 minutes. Add chicken, Parmesan cheese, basil, lemon juice, onion powder, salt, garlic powder and pepper; cook and stir 5 minutes. Remove from heat; stir in cream cheese.

3. Spoon mixture into hollow of each mushroom cap. Bake 10 to 15 minutes or until heated through. Sprinkle with paprika.

Makes about 26 stuffed mushrooms

note

When buying mushrooms, look for mushrooms with firm, smooth, dry caps. Avoid damp, pitted or dried-out mushrooms. Refrigerate unrinsed loose mushrooms in a paper bag or in their original package. Do not soak mushrooms because they absorb water rapidly and turn mushy when you cook them. You can clean mushrooms with a stiff brush without wetting them, or quickly rinse them under a thin stream of cool water. Dry thoroughly with paper towels.

Stuffed Mushroom Caps

Alouette® Garlic and Herb Croustades

- 1 tablespoon olive oil
- ½ cup bacon, diced
- 1 cup baby bella or other mushrooms, chopped
- ⅔ cup chopped roasted red bell pepper
- ½ cup minced onion
- 1 teaspoon chopped garlic
- 1 (6.5-ounce) *or* 2 (4-ounce) packages ALOUETTE® Garlic & Herbs Spreadable Cheese
- 2 tablespoons fresh parsley or 1 tablespoon dried parsley flakes
- 2 (2-ounce) packages mini phyllo shells

In a nonstick pan over medium heat, heat oil and sauté the bacon for 3 to 5 minutes. Add mushrooms, pepper, onion and garlic. Continue sautéing for 3 to 5 minutes. Drain oil from the pan; reduce heat to low and add Alouette®. Blend and simmer for 1 minute. Remove from heat; stir in parsley. Spoon 1 heaping teaspoon into each phyllo shell; serve warm. *Makes 30 appetizers*

Tip: For a creative touch, use any variety of seasonally fresh vegetables such as chopped fennel, summer or winter squash.

Baked Brie

- ½ pound Brie cheese, rind removed
- ¼ cup chopped pecans
- ¼ cup KARO® Dark Corn Syrup

1. Preheat oven to 350°F. Place cheese in shallow oven-safe serving dish. Top with pecans and corn syrup.

2. Bake 8 to 10 minutes or until cheese is almost melted. Serve warm with plain crackers or melba toast. *Makes 8 servings*

Prep Time: 3 minutes
Cook Time: 10 minutes

Alouette® Garlic and Herb Croustades

Beer and Coconut-Macadamia Shrimp

   1 pound large raw shrimp, peeled and deveined, with tails on
1½ teaspoons salt, divided
     Ground red pepper
 ½ cup all-purpose flour
 ¼ teaspoon white pepper
  1 cup sweetened shredded coconut
 ⅔ cup panko (Japanese-style) bread crumbs
 ½ cup finely chopped macadamia nuts
  2 eggs, beaten
 ¼ cup wheat beer
  1 cup peanut oil
    Apricot or pineapple preserves

1. Spread shrimp on paper towels and pat dry. Season with ½ teaspoon salt and red pepper.

2. Combine flour, remaining 1 teaspoon salt and white pepper in shallow dish; set aside. Combine coconut, bread crumbs and macadamia nuts in shallow dish; set aside. Beat eggs and beer in small bowl; set aside.

3. Heat oil in heavy saucepan over medium-high heat to 350°F.

4. Working in small batches, dredge shrimp in flour mixture. Dip in egg mixture and roll in coconut mixture. Place carefully in oil, frying 2 minutes per side. Drain in paper towel-lined baking sheet. Remove extra pieces of coconut from oil with slotted spoon. Fry remaining shrimp.

5. Serve immediately with preserves.   *Makes 6 to 8 servings*

Beer and Coconut-Macadamia Shrimp

Chavrie® Roasted Shallot & Basil Tart

8 shallots or small onions, unpeeled and cut into quarters

3 tablespoons plus 1 teaspoon olive oil

1 sheet frozen puff pastry, thawed

1 large egg, beaten

2 (5.3-ounce) packages CHAVRIE® Goat Milk Cheese, any flavor

¼ cup prepared pesto sauce

¼ cup light cream

3 tablespoons fresh basil, torn into small pieces *or* 1½ teaspoons dried basil

Pinch of salt and black pepper

Preheat oven to 400°F. Brush shallot wedges with 3 tablespoons oil. Brush inside of baking pan lightly with oil. Place shallot wedges flat in a single layer on baking sheet. Bake until shallots are golden on the bottom and very tender, about 15 minutes. Cool in pan.

On lightly floured surface, roll out puff pastry to form a 14×11-inch rectangle. Trim to make edges even. Cut a ½-inch strip from each side and reserve. Rectangle will be 13×10 inches. Place rectangle in a lightly greased baking sheet. Brush edges with some of the beaten egg and reserve remaining egg. Place reserved strips on edges of rectangle on top of beaten egg, forming a border. Trim strips and press gently to adhere. Prick pastry with a fork.

Bake 15 minutes or until edges puff and pastry is golden. Cool completely. In a mixing bowl, beat Chavrie, pesto, cream and 2 tablespoons basil until smooth.

Stir in salt, pepper and remaining egg. Spread Chavrie® mixture evenly over bottom of crust. (If center has puffed, press gently with fingers to level). Remove peel and stem end from roasted shallots and place flat on cheese mixture.

Bake 20 minutes until crust is brown and cheese is set. Cool on rack to room temperature. Sprinkle tart with remaining basil and cut into squares. *Makes 8 servings*

Crab Cakes with Creamy Spicy Remoulade

Crab Cakes

1 stalk celery, finely chopped
1 small onion, finely chopped (⅓ cup)
1 tablespoon olive oil
1 egg, beaten
¼ cup STONYFIELD FARM® Plain LowFat Yogurt
½ teaspoon dry mustard
¼ teaspoon garlic powder
¼ teaspoon onion powder
¼ teaspoon ground red pepper
1½ cups soft French bread crumbs
8 ounces fresh cooked crab meat or canned crab meat, drained, flaked and cartilage removed
3 tablespoons finely chopped red sweet pepper
3 tablespoons finely chopped green sweet pepper
3 tablespoons olive oil

Remoulade

¾ cup STONYFIELD FARM® Plain Lowfat Yogurt
1 scallion, thinly sliced
1 tablespoon chopped fresh flat-leaf parsley
2 teaspoons capers, chopped and drained
2 teaspoons Dijon mustard
1½ teaspoons coarse grain mustard
1 teaspoon tarragon vinegar
¼ teaspoon hot pepper sauce
Salt and freshly ground black pepper, to taste

Crab Cakes

In a skillet, cook celery and onion in 1 tablespoon olive oil until tender. Cool slightly. Combine egg, yogurt, dry mustard, garlic powder, onion powder and ground red pepper in a mixing bowl. Add celery mixture, bread crumbs, crab meat, and the red and green sweet pepper. Mix well. Shape into 12 cakes. Cook the crab cakes in the 3 tablespoons olive oil in a large skillet for 2 to 3 minutes on each side or until lightly browned. Serve with remoulade.

Remoulade

Combine all ingredients in a small mixing bowl. Chill for 30 minutes before serving along side the crab cakes. Keep refrigerated.

Makes 6 servings

Mini Cherry Kugel

4 ounces egg noodles, broken into small pieces (1½ cups)
1 teaspoon salt, divided
4 eggs
1 cup ricotta cheese
½ cup sour cream
½ cup whipping cream
3 tablespoons sugar
½ cup dried sweetened cherries, chopped

1. Preheat oven to 350°F. Coat 12 mini (1¾-inch) muffin cups with nonstick cooking spray.

2. Cook noodles with ½ teaspoon salt according to package directions. Drain well; set aside.

3. Beat eggs, ricotta cheese, sour cream, whipping cream, sugar and remaining ½ teaspoon salt in large bowl with electric mixer at medium speed until blended. Stir in noodles and cherries. Spoon into prepared muffin cups, filling three-fourths full.

4. Bake 50 minutes or until puffed and golden. Cool in pan 1 minute; remove to serving platter. *Makes 12 servings*

note

These mini kugels are basically like a bread pudding with noodles instead of bread. Whether sweet or savory, kugels are very versatile and can be served as a side dish, breakfast treat or a delicious appetizer.

Mini Cherry Kugel

Chicken Meatballs with Chipotle-Honey Sauce

2 pounds ground chicken
2 eggs, lightly beaten
⅓ cup plain dry bread crumbs
⅓ cup chopped fresh cilantro
2 tablespoons fresh lime juice
4 cloves garlic, minced
1 can (4 ounces) chipotle peppers in adobo sauce, divided
1 teaspoon salt
  Chipotle-Honey Sauce (recipe follows)
2 tablespoons vegetable oil

1. Line 2 baking sheets with parchment paper. Combine chicken, eggs, bread crumbs, cilantro, lime juice, garlic, 1 tablespoon adobo sauce and salt in medium bowl; mix well. Form mixture into 48 meatballs. Place meatballs on prepared baking sheets. Cover with plastic wrap; chill 1 hour.

2. Prepare Chipotle-Honey sauce. Preheat oven to 400°F. Brush meatballs with oil. Bake 12 minutes. Transfer meatballs to baking dish. Add sauce; stir until coated. Bake 10 minutes or until meatballs are heated through and glazed with sauce.   *Makes 48 meatballs*

Chipotle-Honey Sauce

¾ cup honey
2 to 3 whole chipotle peppers in adobo sauce
⅓ cup chicken broth
⅓ cup tomato paste
1 tablespoon lime juice
2 teaspoons Dijon mustard
½ teaspoon salt

Combine all ingredients in food processor or blender; process until smooth.   *Makes about 1½ cups*

Chicken Meatballs with Chipotle-Honey Sauce

Oysters Romano

12 oysters, shucked and on the half shell
2 slices bacon, cut into 12 (1-inch) pieces
½ cup Italian seasoned dry bread crumbs
2 tablespoons butter, melted
½ teaspoon garlic salt
6 tablespoons grated Romano or Parmesan cheese
Fresh chives (optional)

1. Preheat oven to 375°F. Place shells with oysters on baking sheet. Top each oyster with 1 piece bacon. Bake 10 minutes or until bacon is crisp.

2. Meanwhile, combine bread crumbs, butter and garlic salt in small bowl. Spoon mixture over oysters; sprinkle with cheese. Bake 5 to 10 minutes or until cheese melts. Garnish with chives.

Makes 12 oysters

Prosciutto-Wrapped Figs with Orange-Honey Sauce

16 dried mission figs
8 slices prosciutto, at room temperature
6 tablespoons orange juice
1 tablespoon honey
2 teaspoons lemon juice
⅛ teaspoon red pepper flakes
Salt (optional)

1. Place figs in small saucepan; cover with water. Bring to a boil over medium-high heat. Reduce heat; cover and simmer 8 minutes or until figs are soft. Drain; set aside to cool.

2. Meanwhile, cut prosciutto slices in half lengthwise. Wrap each fig with prosciutto strip; secure with toothpick. Arrange on serving plate.

3. Combine orange juice, honey, lemon juice, red pepper flakes and salt, if desired, in small saucepan. Bring to a boil over medium-high heat. Cook 2 minutes or until mixture is syrupy and reduced by half. Drizzle sauce over figs or serve for dipping.   *Makes 8 servings*

Oysters Romano

Turkey Canapés

8 slices JENNIE-O TURKEY STORE® Turkey Pastrami, turkey salami or turkey ham

32 buttery round crackers, wheat crackers or rye crackers

¾ cup (6 ounces) cream cheese with chives or herb-flavored cream cheese

1 small cucumber

Fresh dill (optional)

Cut each slice of turkey into quarters; set aside. Spread each cracker with about 1 teaspoon cream cheese. Fold turkey quarters in half. Place turkey on cream cheese. Cut cucumber lengthwise in half; cut each half into ¼-inch slices. Top each cracker with cucumber slice and garnish with fresh dill, if desired.

Makes 32 canapés

Prep Time: 30 minutes

Prosciutto Roll-Ups

1 container (5 ounces) herb lettuce mix or baby mixed greens, washed and dried

2 to 4 tablespoons balsamic or red wine vinegar salad dressing

½ pound (about 24 thin slices) prosciutto or ham

1. Combine greens and salad dressing in medium bowl; toss to coat.

2. Place ½ cup greens at one end of prosciutto slice. Roll up tightly, starting at short end. Place on serving platter, seam side down. Cover and refrigerate until serving. *Makes 24 roll-ups*

Tip: Substitute balsamic or fig balsamic vinegar for salad dressing.

Turkey Canapés

Smoked Salmon Roses

   1 package (8 ounces) cream cheese, softened
   1 tablespoon prepared horseradish
   1 tablespoon minced fresh dill
   1 tablespoon half-and-half
  16 slices (12 to 16 ounces) smoked salmon
   1 red bell pepper, cut into thin strips
     Fresh dill sprigs

1. Combine cream cheese, horseradish, minced dill and half-and-half in small bowl. Beat until light and creamy.

2. Spread 1 tablespoon cream cheese mixture over each salmon slice. Roll up jelly-roll style. Slice each roll in half crosswise. Arrange salmon rolls, cut sides down, on serving dish to resemble roses. Place pepper strips and dill sprig in center of each rose.

Makes 32 roses

Classic Shrimp Cocktail

  6 cups water
  2 tablespoons HERB-OX® chicken flavored bouillon
  1 stalk celery, cut into 1-inch pieces
  2 bay leaves
  1 lemon, cut into quarters
  2 pounds fresh shrimp
    Cocktail sauce

In large stockpot, bring water, bouillon, celery, bay leaves and lemons to a boil. Add shrimp and cook for 3 to 5 minutes or until cooked through. Drain and cool under cold water. Chill until ready to serve. To serve, peel and devein shrimp, if desired. Serve with cocktail sauce.

Makes 8 servings

Serving Suggestion: Serve shrimp over the edge of a rimmed glass filled with cocktail sauce.

Smoked Salmon Roses

international
bests

Fish Bites with Romesco Sauce

1 plum tomato, quartered
1 slice crusty Italian bread
3 tablespoons whole blanched almonds
2 cloves garlic
2 tablespoons chopped pimiento, drained
1 tablespoon red wine vinegar
¼ teaspoon paprika
¼ teaspoon plus ⅛ teaspoon salt, divided
1 egg white
2 tablespoons all-purpose flour
½ teaspoon ground red pepper
⅓ cup ground almonds
½ pound tilapia fillets

1. Preheat oven to 350°F. Lightly grease two baking sheets; set aside.

2. For sauce, place tomato, bread, whole almonds and garlic on one baking sheet. Bake 12 to 15 minutes or until almonds are lightly browned. Transfer ingredients to food processor; process using on/off pulsing action just until ingredients are coarsely chopped. Add pimiento, vinegar, paprika and ⅛ teaspoon salt. Process until almost smooth. Place sauce in small bowl; set aside.

3. Lightly beat egg white in small bowl. Combine flour, red pepper and ¼ teaspoon salt in shallow bowl. Place ground almonds in another shallow bowl.

continued on page 80

Fish Bites with Romesco Sauce, continued

4. Cut tilapia fillets into four 1½-inch pieces. Coat fish in flour, shaking off excess. Dip into egg white; roll in almonds until evenly coated.

5. Arrange fish on second baking sheet. Bake 18 to 20 minutes or until fish is golden brown and begins to flake when tested with fork. Serve immediately with sauce.   *Makes 4 servings*

Note: Slivered almonds can be substituted for the whole almonds. In step 2, bake them on a separate baking pan for 8 minutes or until lightly browned, stirring once.

Savory Bruschetta

   ¼ **cup olive oil**
   1 **clove garlic, minced**
   1 **loaf (1 pound) French bread, cut in half lengthwise**
   1 **package (8 ounces) PHILADELPHIA® Cream Cheese, softened**
   3 **tablespoons KRAFT® 100% Grated Parmesan Cheese**
   2 **tablespoons chopped pitted ripe olives**
   1 **cup chopped plum tomatoes**
   ¼ **cup chopped fresh basil**

PREHEAT oven to 400°F. Mix oil and garlic; spread on cut surfaces of bread. Bake 8 to 10 minutes or until lightly browned. Cool.

MIX cream cheese and Parmesan cheese with electric mixer on medium speed until blended. Stir in olives.

SPREAD toasted bread halves with cream cheese mixture; top with tomatoes. Cut into 24 slices to serve. Sprinkle with basil.
                     Makes 2 dozen or 24 servings, 1 slice each

Shortcut: Prepare as directed, using 1 can (14½ ounces) diced tomatoes, drained, for the chopped fresh tomatoes.

Prep Time: 15 minutes
Bake Time: 10 minutes

Savory Bruschetta

Fiesta Cilantro Fondue

1 can (10¾ ounces) CAMPBELL'S® Condensed Creamy
    Chicken Verde Soup

¼ cup beer

½ cup PACE® Cilantro Chunky Salsa

2 cups shredded Cheddar cheese (8 ounces)

Suggested Dippers

Assorted PEPPERIDGE FARM® Crackers, French bread cubes, cooked
breaded chicken nuggets, steamed vegetables (asparagus
spears, broccoli flowerets, red potato wedges) and/or tortilla
chips

1. Mix the soup and beer in a 1-quart saucepan. Bring to a boil over medium heat. Stir in the salsa and the cheese. Heat through until the cheese melts, stirring occasionally.

2. Pour the sauce into a fondue pot or slow cooker.

3. Serve warm with *Suggested Dippers*.   *Makes 2 cups*

Prep Time: 5 minutes
Cook Time: 10 minutes

note

*Ready in just 15 minutes, this fondue will be a huge hit for
a fiesta or any casual party. When serving, keep the fondue warm
over as low heat as possible to avoid scorching the cheese.*

Fiesta Cilantro Fondue

Spanish Tortilla

1 teaspoon olive oil
1 cup thinly sliced peeled potato
1 small zucchini, thinly sliced
¼ cup chopped onion
1 clove garlic, minced
1 cup shredded cooked chicken
8 eggs
½ teaspoon salt
½ teaspoon black pepper
¼ teaspoon red pepper flakes
   Fresh tomato salsa (optional)

1. Heat oil in 10-inch nonstick skillet over medium-high heat. Add potato, zucchini, onion and garlic; cook and stir about 5 minutes or until potato is tender, turning frequently. Stir in chicken; cook 1 minute.

2. Meanwhile, whisk eggs, salt, pepper and red pepper flakes in large bowl. Carefully pour egg mixture into skillet. Reduce heat to low. Cover and cook 12 to 15 minutes or until egg mixture is set in center.

3. Loosen edges of tortilla and slide onto large serving platter. Let stand 5 minutes before cutting into wedges or 1-inch cubes. Serve warm or at room temperature. Serve with salsa, if desired.

Makes 10 to 12 servings

Spanish Tortilla

Ginger Plum Spareribs

1 jar (10 ounces) damson plum preserves or apple jelly
⅓ cup KARO® Light or Dark Corn Syrup
⅓ cup soy sauce
¼ cup chopped green onions
2 cloves garlic, minced
2 teaspoons ground ginger
2 pounds pork spareribs, trimmed, cut into serving pieces

1. In small saucepan combine preserves, corn syrup, soy sauce, green onions, garlic and ginger. Stirring constantly, cook over medium heat until melted and smooth.

2. Pour into 11×7×2-inch baking dish. Add ribs, turning to coat. Cover; refrigerate several hours or overnight, turning once.

3. Remove ribs from marinade; place on rack in shallow baking pan.

4. Bake in 350°F oven about 1 hour or until tender, turning occasionally and basting with marinade. Do not baste during last 5 minutes of cooking.   *Makes about 20 appetizers*

Ginger Plum Chicken Wings: Omit spareribs. Follow recipe for Ginger Plum Spareribs. Use 2½ pounds chicken wings, separated at the joints (tips discarded). Bake 45 minutes, basting with marinade during last 30 minutes.

Prep Time: 15 minutes, plus marinating
Bake Time: 1 hour

Ginger Plum Spareribs

Mini Egg Rolls

½ pound ground pork
3 cloves garlic, minced
1 teaspoon minced fresh ginger
¼ teaspoon red pepper flakes
6 cups (12 ounces) shredded coleslaw mix
¼ cup reduced-sodium soy sauce
1 tablespoon cornstarch
1 tablespoon seasoned rice vinegar
½ cup chopped green onions
28 wonton wrappers
Peanut or canola oil for frying
Sweet and sour sauce
Chinese hot mustard

1. Combine pork, garlic, ginger and red pepper flakes in large nonstick skillet. Cook over medium heat, stirring to break up meat, about 4 minutes or until pork is cooked through. Add coleslaw mix; cover and cook 2 minutes. Uncover and cook 2 minutes or until coleslaw mix is wilted but crisp-tender.

2. Combine soy sauce and cornstarch in small bowl; mix well. Stir into pork mixture. Add vinegar; cook 2 to 3 minutes or until sauce thickens. Remove from heat; stir in green onions.

3. To fill egg rolls, place one wonton wrapper on clean work surface with one point facing you. Spoon 1 level tablespoon pork mixture across and just below center of wrapper. Fold bottom point of wrapper up over filling; fold side points over filling, forming envelope shape. Moisten inside edges of top point with water and roll egg roll toward top point, pressing firmly to seal. Repeat with remaining wrappers and filling.

4. Heat about ¼ inch oil in large skillet over medium heat; fry egg rolls in small batches about 2 minutes per side or until golden brown. Drain on paper towels. Serve warm with sweet and sour sauce and hot mustard.

Makes 28 mini egg rolls

Mini Egg Rolls

Pork Empanaditas (Mini Turnovers)

¾ pound ground pork
1 small onion, finely chopped
2 cloves garlic, crushed
3 tablespoons *Frank's® RedHot®* Original Cayenne Pepper Sauce
1 tablespoon *French's®* Worcestershire Sauce
2 teaspoons chili powder
½ teaspoon ground thyme
½ cup chopped fresh parsley
2 refrigerated pie crust sheets (9 inches)
1 egg plus 2 tablespoons water, beaten
   Sesame seeds

1. Cook and stir pork, onion and garlic in large nonstick skillet over medium heat until meat is no longer pink; drain fat. Add **Frank's RedHot** Sauce, Worcestershire, chili powder and thyme. Cook 3 minutes, stirring occasionally. Stir in parsley. Cool 10 minutes.

2. Preheat oven to 375°F. Line baking sheets with foil; grease foil. Roll each pie crust sheet into 13-inch circle on lightly floured surface. Cut into rounds using a 4-inch cookie cutter.* Brush edges of each round with egg mixture. Spoon 1 tablespoon pork mixture into center of each round. Fold rounds in half, pressing edges to seal.

3. Place filled rounds onto baking sheets. Prick tops with fork; brush lightly with remaining egg mixture. Sprinkle with sesame seeds. Re-roll pastry scraps; cut and fill with remaining pork mixture.

4. Bake 20 minutes or until golden. Serve warm.

Makes about 18 empanaditas

*Or, use an empty 28-ounce can for 4-inch cookie cutter.

Prep Time: 30 minutes
Bake Time: 20 minutes

Falafel Nuggets

Falafel

2 cans (15 ounces each) chickpeas
½ cup whole wheat flour
½ cup chopped fresh parsley
⅓ cup lemon juice
¼ cup minced onion
2 tablespoons minced garlic
2 teaspoons ground cumin
½ teaspoon salt
½ teaspoon ground red pepper or red pepper flakes
½ cup canola oil

Sauce

2½ cups tomato sauce
⅓ cup tomato paste
2 tablespoons lemon juice
2 teaspoons sugar
1 teaspoon dry onion powder
½ teaspoon salt

1. Preheat oven to 400°F. Coat baking sheet with nonstick cooking spray.

2. To make falafel, drain chickpeas, reserving ¼ cup liquid. Combine chickpeas, reserved liquid, flour, parsley, ⅓ cup lemon juice, onion, garlic, cumin, ½ teaspoon salt and red pepper in food processor or blender. Process until well blended. Shape mixture into 36 (1-inch) balls; place 1 to 2 inches apart on baking sheet. Refrigerate 15 minutes.

3. Meanwhile, to make sauce, combine all ingredients in medium saucepan. Simmer over medium-low heat 20 minutes.

4. Heat oil in large nonstick skillet over medium-high heat. Fry falafel in batches until browned. Place on baking sheet; bake 8 to 10 minutes. Serve with warm sauce.   *Makes 36 nuggets*

Hint: Falafel also can be baked completely to reduce fat content. Spray balls lightly with nonstick cooking spray and bake on baking sheet 15 to 20 minutes, turning once.

Chicken Satay Skewers

    6 garlic cloves, chopped
    4 teaspoons dried coriander
    4 teaspoons light brown sugar
    2 teaspoons salt
 1½ teaspoons HERSHEY'S Cocoa
    1 teaspoon ground black pepper
  ½ cup soy sauce
    6 tablespoons vegetable oil
    2 tablespoons lime juice
    4 teaspoons fresh chopped ginger
 2½ pounds boneless, skinless chicken breasts
       Peanut Dipping Sauce (recipe follows)
  ¼ cup fresh cilantro, chopped (optional)

1. Combine garlic, coriander, brown sugar, salt, cocoa and pepper in large bowl. Stir in soy sauce, oil, lime juice and ginger. Cut chicken into 1½- to 2-inch cubes. Add to soy sauce mixture, stirring to coat. Cover; marinate in refrigerator for at least 2 hours.

2. Meanwhile, prepare Peanut Dipping Sauce. Thread chicken pieces onto skewers. Grill or broil, basting with marinade. Discard leftover marinade. Garnish with chopped cilantro, if desired. Serve with Peanut Dipping Sauce. Refrigerate leftovers.

Makes 15 to 20 skewers

Peanut Dipping Sauce

  ½ cup peanut oil
    1 cup REESE'S® Creamy Peanut Butter
  ¼ cup lime juice
  ¼ cup soy sauce
    3 tablespoons honey
    2 garlic cloves, minced
    1 teaspoon cayenne pepper
  ½ teaspoon hot pepper sauce

Whisk oil into peanut butter in medium bowl. Blend in lime juice, soy sauce, honey, garlic, cayenne pepper and hot pepper sauce. Adjust flavors to taste for a sweet/hot flavor. *Makes 2¼ cups*

Chicken Satay Skewers

Manchego Cheese Croquettes

¼ **cup (½ stick) butter**
1 **tablespoon minced shallot or onion**
½ **cup all-purpose flour**
¾ **cup milk**
½ **cup grated manchego cheese or Parmesan cheese, divided**
¼ **teaspoon salt**
¼ **teaspoon smoked paprika or paprika**
⅛ **teaspoon ground nutmeg**
1 **egg**
½ **cup bread crumbs**
Vegetable oil

1. Melt butter in medium skillet over medium heat. Add shallot; cook and stir 2 minutes. Stir in flour; cook and stir 2 minutes. Gradually whisk in milk; cook until mixture comes to a boil. Remove from heat. Stir in ¼ cup cheese, salt, paprika and nutmeg.

2. Transfer mixture to small bowl; cover and refrigerate several hours or up to 24 hours.

3. Shape teaspoonfuls of dough into 1-inch balls with lightly floured hands.

4. Beat egg in shallow bowl. Combine bread crumbs and remaining ¼ cup cheese in second shallow bowl. Dip each ball into egg, then roll in bread crumb mixture.

5. Heat ¼ cup oil in medium skillet over medium-high heat. Cook croquettes in batches until brown on all sides, replenishing oil as needed. Drain on paper towels. Serve warm.   *Makes 6 servings*

Note: Cooked croquettes may be kept warm in a 200°F oven up to 30 minutes before serving.

Manchego Cheese Croquettes

Spanish Tapas Potatoes (Patatas Bravas)

2½ pounds small red potatoes, quartered
⅓ cup plus 2 tablespoons olive oil, divided
1 teaspoon coarse or kosher salt
½ teaspoon dried rosemary
1 can (about 14 ounces) diced tomatoes
2 tablespoons red wine vinegar
1 tablespoon minced garlic
1 tablespoon chili powder
1 tablespoon paprika
¼ teaspoon salt
¼ teaspoon ground chipotle pepper
⅛ to ¼ teaspoon ground red pepper

1. Preheat oven to 425°F.

2. For potatoes, combine potatoes, 2 tablespoons oil, coarse salt and rosemary in large bowl; toss to coat. Spread mixture in large shallow baking pan. Roast potatoes 35 to 40 minutes or until crisp and brown, turning every 10 minutes.

3. For sauce, combine tomatoes, ⅓ cup oil, vinegar, garlic, chili powder, paprika, ¼ teaspoon salt, chipotle pepper and red pepper in blender or food processor. Process just until blended. Transfer to large saucepan. Cover; cook over medium-high heat 5 minutes or until slightly thickened. Cool.

4. To serve, drizzle sauce over potatoes or serve sauce in separate bowl for dipping. *Makes 10 to 12 servings*

Note: Sauce can be made up to 24 hours ahead of time. Cover and refrigerate. Bring to room temperature or reheat before serving.

Spanish Tapas Potatoes

Baked Crab Rangoon

1 can (6 ounces) white crabmeat, drained, flaked
4 ounces (½ of 8-ounce package) PHILADELPHIA® Neufchâtel Cheese, ⅓ **Less Fat than Cream Cheese, softened**
¼ **cup thinly sliced green onions**
¼ **cup KRAFT® Mayo Light Mayonnaise**
12 wonton wrappers

PREHEAT oven to 350°F. Mix crabmeat, Neufchâtel cheese, onions and mayo.

SPRAY 12 (2½-inch) muffin cups with cooking spray. Gently place 1 wonton wrapper in each cup, allowing edges of wrappers to extend above sides of cups. Fill evenly with crabmeat mixture.

BAKE 18 to 20 minutes or until edges are golden brown and filling is heated through. Serve warm. Garnish with sliced green onions, if desired. *Makes 12 servings, 1 wonton each*

Food Facts: Wonton wrappers are usually found in the grocery store in the refrigerated section of the produce department.

For Mini Crab Rangoons: Use 24 wonton wrappers. Gently place 1 wonton wrapper in each of 24 miniature muffin cups sprayed with cooking spray. Fill evenly with crabmeat mixture and bake as directed. Makes 12 servings, 2 wontons each.

Prep Time: 20 minutes
Bake Time: 20 minutes

Baked Crab Rangoon

Chinese Crab Cakes

1 pound fresh* or canned pasteurized lump crabmeat
½ cup plus ⅓ cup panko bread crumbs, divided
2 eggs
2 green onions, finely chopped
1 tablespoon dark sesame oil
1 tablespoon grated fresh ginger
1 tablespoon Chinese hot mustard
2 tablespoons peanut or canola oil, divided
½ cup sweet and sour sauce

Choose special grade crabmeat for this recipe. It is less expensive and already flaked but just as flavorful as backfin, lump or claw meat. Look for it in the refrigerated seafood section of the supermarket. Shelf-stable canned crabmeat can be substituted.

1. Combine crabmeat, ½ cup panko, eggs, green onions, sesame oil, ginger and mustard in large bowl; mix well.

2. Shape level ⅓ cupfuls of mixture into 8 patties about ½ inch thick. (At this point patties may be covered and chilled up to 2 hours.)

3. Heat 1 tablespoon peanut oil in large nonstick skillet over medium heat. Place remaining ⅓ cup panko in shallow dish; dip each crab cake lightly in panko to coat.

4. Add 4 crab cakes to skillet. Cook 3 to 4 minutes per side or until golden brown and heated through, turning carefully. Keep warm. Repeat with remaining 1 tablespoon oil and 4 crab cakes. Serve with sweet and sour sauce. *Makes 8 crab cakes*

Chinese Crab Cakes

Pesto Chicken-Fontina Crostini

1 baguette, cut into 30 (¼-inch-thick) slices
½ (16-ounce) package PERDUE® Fit 'N Easy® Thin Sliced Skinless & Boneless Chicken Breast or Turkey Breast Cutlets, cut into 30 pieces (8 ounces)
1 tablespoon prepared pesto
¼ teaspoon red pepper flakes
6 ounces fontina, cut into 30 pieces
½ cup roasted red peppers, cut into 1-inch pieces
30 small fresh basil leaves for garnish

Preheat oven to 400°F. Place baguette slices on a baking sheet and toast until golden.

Spray a nonstick skillet with olive oil cooking spray and warm over high heat. Add chicken and sauté until firm and golden. Stir in pesto and red pepper flakes. Set aside.

Place a piece of fontina on each baguette slice and return to oven until cheese melts. Top each crostini with a piece of chicken and a piece of roasted pepper. Garnish with basil leaves and serve.

Makes 30 crostini

Prep Time: 30 minutes
Cook Time: 10 minutes

Crostini are simply small, thin slices of toasted bread.
For added flavor, brush the toasts with olive oil and rub with
garlic cloves before topping with the chicken.

Classic Antipasto Italiano

- 8 large romaine lettuce leaves
- 2 large yellow, orange and/or red tomatoes, sliced
- 1 (2-ounce) jar whole drained pepperoncini
- 4 ounces thinly sliced prosciutto or ham
- 8 ounces bocconcini (fresh mozzarella cheese balls)
- 1 (8-ounce) jar roasted tri-color or red peppers, drained and thinly sliced
- ¼ cup oil-cured olives
- ¼ cup very thinly sliced red onion
- 30 sprays WISH-BONE® SALAD SPRITZERS® Red Wine Mist Cabernet Vinaigrette Dressing

1. On serving platter, arrange lettuce. In center of lettuce, arrange tomatoes and pepperoncini, then prosciutto. Arrange remaining ingredients around prosciutto.

2. Just before serving, spritz with WISH-BONE® SALAD SPRITZERS® Red Wine Mist Cabernet Vinaigrette Dressing.   *Makes 6 servings*

Prep Time: 20 minutes

note

A classic antipasto is a great menu option that will leave you with more time for socializing with friends and family. The antipasto tray can be prepared ahead of time and stored in the refrigerator. Spritz with dressing just before serving.

Caponata Appetizers

1 tablespoon vegetable oil
1 large eggplant, cut in cubes (about 8 cups)
1 Spanish onion, chopped (about 2 cups)
1 large red pepper, chopped (about 1 cup)
2 cloves garlic, minced
1 can (10¾ ounces) CAMPBELL'S® Condensed Tomato Soup
1⅓ cups water
1 teaspoon dried oregano leaves, crushed
    PEPPERIDGE FARM® Cracker Quartet *or* Cracker Trio Entertaining
    Collection Cracker Assortment

1. Heat the oil in a 6-quart saucepot over medium-high heat. Add the eggplant, onion, pepper and garlic and cook for 10 minutes or until the eggplant begins to soften.

2. Stir in the soup and water and heat the mixture to a boil. Cover and reduce the heat to low. Cook for 40 minutes more or until the vegetables are tender.

3. Stir in the oregano. Serve warm or at room temperature with the crackers. *Makes 5 cups*

Leftover Tip: Leftover caponata is delicious tossed with hot cooked pasta topped off with some grated Parmesan cheese.

Prep Time: 15 minutes
Cook Time: 45 minutes

Caponata Appetizers

Chipotle Chicken Quesadillas

1 package (8 ounces) cream cheese, softened
1 cup (4 ounces) shredded Mexican cheese blend
1 tablespoon minced chipotle pepper in adobo sauce
5 (10-inch) flour tortillas
5 cups shredded cooked chicken (about 1¼ pounds)
Nonstick cooking spray
Guacamole, sour cream, salsa and chopped fresh cilantro

1. Combine cheeses and pepper in large bowl.

2. Spread ⅓ cup cheese mixture over half of one tortilla. Top with about 1 cup chicken. Fold over tortilla. Repeat with remaining tortillas.

3. Heat large nonstick skillet over medium-high heat. Spray outside surface of each tortilla with cooking spray. Cook tortillas 4 to 6 minutes or until lightly browned, turning once during cooking.

4. Cut each tortilla into 4 wedges. Serve with guacamole, sour cream, salsa and cilantro.   *Makes 20 wedges*

Tip: Chipotle peppers in adobo sauce can be found in small cans in the Mexican food section of the supermarket.

Bacon-Wrapped Dates

1 container (12 ounces) whole Medjool dates
1 pound thick-cut bacon (about 11 slices)

1. Preheat oven to 450°F. Line shallow baking pan or baking sheet with parchment paper. To remove pits from dates, cut tips off each end of date. Insert flat end of wooden skewer into each date and push out pit.

2. Cut bacon slices lengthwise into halves. Wrap each date with slice of bacon; secure bacon with toothpick.

3. Arrange dates in prepared baking pan, spacing at least 1 inch apart. Bake 18 to 20 minutes turning after 10 minutes until bacon is cooked. Discard toothpicks before serving.

Makes 8 to 10 servings

Chipotle Chicken Quesadillas

Chorizo & Caramelized Onion Tortilla

¼ **cup olive oil**
3 **medium yellow onions, quartered and sliced**
½ **pound Spanish chorizo (about 2 links) or andouille sausage, diced**
6 **eggs**
  Salt and black pepper
½ **cup chopped fresh parsley**

1. Preheat oven to 350°F. Spray 9-inch square baking pan with olive oil cooking spray.

2. Heat oil in medium skillet over medium heat. Add onions; cook, covered, 10 minutes or until onions are translucent. Reduce heat to low; cook, uncovered, 40 minutes or until golden and very tender. Remove onions from skillet and set aside to cool.

3. Add chorizo to same skillet. Cook over medium heat, stirring occasionally, 5 minutes or until chorizo just begins to brown. Remove chorizo from skillet; set aside to cool.

4. Whisk eggs in medium bowl; season with salt and pepper. Add onions, chorizo and parsley; stir gently until well blended. Pour egg mixture into prepared pan.

5. Bake 12 to 15 minutes or until center is almost set. *Turn oven to broil.* Broil 1 to 2 minutes or until top just starts to brown. Transfer pan to wire rack; cool completely. Cut into 36 squares; serve on wooden toothpicks cold or at room temperature.   *Makes 36 squares*

note

The tortilla can be made up to 1 day ahead and refrigerated until serving. To serve at room temperature, remove from refrigerator 30 minutes before serving.

Chorizo & Caramelized Onion Tortilla

super vegetarian nibbles

Grilled Vegetable Pizzas

2 tablespoons olive oil

1 clove garlic, minced

1 medium red bell pepper, halved and seeded

2 (½-inch-thick) slices eggplant, lightly salted

1 (½-inch-thick) slice red onion

4 small (6-inch) prebaked pizza crusts

4 teaspoons prepared pesto sauce

1¼ cups grated CABOT® Sharp Cheddar (about 5 ounces), divided

1. Preheat barbecue grill, allowing coals to turn to gray ash, or set gas grill to medium.

2. In small bowl, combine olive oil and garlic. Place vegetables on grill and cook, brushing with oil-garlic mixture and turning frequently, until lightly browned and tender, about 10 minutes.

3. Remove vegetables from grill, let cool slightly and cut into ½-inch pieces.

4. Place pizza crusts on grill, top side down, and cook 3 to 5 minutes or until warm.

5. Remove crusts from grill and spread each with 1 teaspoon pesto sauce. Top each with ¼ cup cheese and one fourth of vegetables. Scatter remaining ¼ cup cheese on tops.

6. Return pizzas to grill and cook until crust is crisp and cheese is melted. Cut pizzas into wedges and serve.   *Makes 4 pizzas*

Fried Tofu with Sesame Dipping Sauce

3 tablespoons soy sauce or tamari
2 tablespoons unseasoned rice wine vinegar
2 teaspoons sugar
1 teaspoon sesame seeds, toasted*
1 teaspoon dark sesame oil
⅛ teaspoon red pepper flakes
1 block (about 12 ounces) extra firm tofu
2 tablespoons all-purpose flour
1 egg
¾ cup panko bread crumbs
4 tablespoons vegetable oil, divided

To toast sesame seeds, spread seeds in small skillet. Shake skillet over medium-low heat until seeds begin to pop and turn golden, about 3 minutes.

1. For dipping sauce, combine soy sauce, vinegar, sugar, sesame seeds, sesame oil and red pepper flakes in small bowl. Set aside.

2. Drain tofu and press between paper towels to remove excess water. Cut crosswise into 4 slices; cut each slice diagonally into triangles. Place flour in shallow dish. Beat egg in shallow bowl. Place panko in another shallow bowl.

3. Dip each piece of tofu lightly in flour on all sides, then in egg, turning to coat. Drain and roll in panko to coat lightly.

4. Heat 2 tablespoons vegetable oil in large nonstick skillet over high heat. Reduce heat to medium; add tofu in single layer. Cook 1 to 2 minutes per side or until golden brown. Repeat with remaining tofu. Serve with dipping sauce.   *Makes 4 servings*

note

Panko bread crumbs are used in Japanese cooking to provide a crisp exterior to fried foods. They are coarser than ordinary bread crumbs. You'll find panko in the Asian aisle of large supermarkets.

Fried Tofu with Sesame Dipping Sauce

Onion & White Bean Spread

1 can (about 15 ounces) cannellini or Great Northern beans, rinsed and drained

¼ cup grated Parmesan cheese

¼ cup chopped green onions

¼ cup olive oil

1 tablespoon fresh rosemary leaves, chopped

2 cloves garlic, minced

Additional olive oil

French bread slices

1. Combine beans, Parmesan, green onions, oil, rosemary and garlic in food processor; process 30 to 40 seconds or until mixture is almost smooth.

2. Spoon bean mixture into serving bowl. Drizzle additional olive oil over spread just before serving. Serve with bread.

Makes 1¼ cups spread

For a more rustic-looking spread, place all ingredients in a medium bowl and mash them with a potato masher.

Onion & White Bean Spread

Roasted Corn Salsa

4 ears corn in husks (about 2 pounds)
1 tablespoon vegetable oil
2 cups chopped yellow onion
2 teaspoons ground cumin
1 teaspoon red pepper flakes *or* **1 to 2 tablespoons minced fresh chilies**
2 cups chopped tomatoes
1 cup sliced black olives
½ cup coarsely chopped fresh cilantro leaves
¼ cup freshly squeezed lime juice
1 teaspoon sugar
2 to 3 teaspoons diced chipotle peppers, canned in adobo sauce
1 to 2 teaspoons adobo sauce from canned chipotles
½ teaspoon salt

Husk corn and cut kernels from cob using long-bladed knife. Heat oil in large skillet over high heat. Add corn and sauté for about 2 minutes or until it gets some golden patches. Add onion and sauté 1 minute longer; stir in cumin and red pepper flakes. Remove from heat and combine with all other ingredients in bowl.

Makes about 5 cups

Favorite recipe from **National Onion Association**

Pastry Shells with Bel Paese® and Mushrooms

8 ounces fresh mushrooms, cleaned and sliced
1 clove garlic, minced
3 to 4 tablespoons olive oil
2 teaspoons all-purpose flour
½ cup half-and-half
2 tablespoons minced fresh parsley
¼ teaspoon salt
    Dash pepper
4 ounces BEL PAESE® cheese,* cut into small pieces
8 ready-to-eat pastry shells or frozen pastry shells,** baked

Remove wax coating and moist, white crust from cheese.

**Ready-to-eat pastry shells and frozen shells are available in bakeries, gourmet shops and specialty sections of supermarkets. These shells should not be sweet.*

Preheat oven to 350°F. In small skillet, cook and stir mushrooms and garlic in olive oil over medium heat until mushrooms are tender. Stir in flour, half-and-half, parsley, salt and pepper. Remove from heat.

Arrange pastry shells on baking sheet. Line shells with half the Bel Paese® cheese. Spoon sauce over cheese. Top with remaining cheese. Bake until cheese melts, 3 to 4 minutes.   *Makes 8 shells*

Two-Tomato Kalamata Crostini

8 sun-dried tomatoes (not packed in oil)
1 baguette (4 ounces), cut into 20 (¼-inch-thick) slices
5 ounces grape tomatoes, chopped
12 kalamata olives, pitted and finely chopped
2 teaspoons cider vinegar
1½ teaspoons dried basil
1 teaspoon extra-virgin olive oil
⅛ teaspoon salt
1 clove garlic, halved crosswise

1. Preheat oven to 350°F. Place sun-dried tomatoes in small bowl; cover with boiling water. Let stand 10 minutes. Drain; chop tomatoes.

2. Place bread slices on large baking sheet. Bake 10 minutes or until golden brown around edges. Cool on wire rack.

3. Meanwhile, combine grape tomatoes, sun-dried tomatoes, olives, vinegar, basil, oil and salt in medium bowl; mix well.

4. Rub bread slices with garlic. Top each bread slice with 1 tablespoon tomato mixture.   *Makes 20 servings*

Tip: Use a serrated knife to slice bread and tomatoes.

Two-Tomato Kalamata Crostini

Chile 'n' Cheese Spirals

4 ounces cream cheese, softened
1 cup (4 ounces) shredded cheddar cheese
1 can (4 ounces) ORTEGA® Diced Green Chiles
3 green onions, sliced
½ cup chopped red bell pepper
1 can (2.25 ounces) chopped ripe olives
4 (8-inch) taco-size flour tortillas
   ORTEGA® Salsa, any variety

COMBINE cream cheese, cheddar cheese, chiles, green onions, pepper and olives in medium bowl.

SPREAD ½ cup cheese mixture on each tortilla; roll up. Wrap each roll in plastic wrap; chill for 1 hour.

REMOVE plastic wrap; slice each roll into six ¾-inch pieces. Serve with salsa for dipping.   *Makes 24 appetizers*

Chile 'n' Cheese Spirals can be prepared and kept in the refrigerator for 1 to 2 days.

Chile 'n' Cheese Spirals

Spicy Roasted Chickpeas

1 can (about 20 ounces) chickpeas, rinsed and drained
3 tablespoons olive oil
½ teaspoon salt
½ teaspoon black pepper
¾ to 1 tablespoon chili powder
⅛ to ¼ teaspoon ground red pepper
1 lime, cut into wedges

1. Preheat oven to 400°F. .

2. Combine chickpeas, olive oil, salt and black pepper on large baking sheet; stir to coat. Arrange in single layer. Bake 15 minutes or until chickpeas begin to brown, stirring twice.

3. Sprinkle with chili powder and red pepper; bake 5 minutes or until dark golden-red. Serve with lime wedges.

Makes 1 cup chickpeas

Pesto-Stuffed Mushrooms

12 medium mushrooms
⅔ cup basil pesto
¼ cup (1 ounce) grated Parmesan cheese
¼ cup chopped roasted red pepper
3 tablespoons seasoned dry bread crumbs
3 tablespoons pine nuts
¼ cup (1 ounce) shredded mozzarella cheese

1. Preheat oven to 400°F. Remove mushroom stems; reserve for another use. Place mushroom caps, stem side up, on ungreased baking sheet.

2. Combine pesto, Parmesan cheese, red pepper, bread crumbs and pine nuts in small bowl; stir until well blended.

3. Fill mushroom caps with pesto mixture. Sprinkle with mozzarella cheese. Bake 8 to 10 minutes or until filling is hot and cheese is melted. Serve immediately. *Makes 12 mushrooms*

Spicy Roasted Chickpeas

Edamame Hummus

1 package (16 ounces) frozen shelled edamame, thawed
2 green onions, chopped (about ½ cup)
½ cup loosely packed fresh cilantro
3 to 4 tablespoons water
2 tablespoons canola oil
1½ tablespoons fresh lime juice
1 tablespoon honey
2 cloves garlic
1 teaspoon salt
¼ teaspoon black pepper
Rice crackers, baby carrots, cucumber slices and sugar snap peas

1. Place edamame, green onions, cilantro, 3 tablespoons water, oil, lime juice, honey, garlic, salt and pepper in food processor; process until smooth. Add additional water if necessary to thin dip.

2. Serve with crackers and vegetables for dipping. Store leftover dip in refrigerator for up to 4 days. *Makes about 2 cups*

note

Edamame, also called green soybeans, are immature soybeans that are picked while still green and sweet. They are sold both whole (in their pods) and shelled. Look for shelled edamame in the freezer section of your supermarket.

Edamame Hummus

Mexican Roll-Ups

6 uncooked lasagna noodles
¾ cup prepared guacamole
¾ cup chunky salsa
¾ cup (3 ounces) shredded Cheddar cheese
Additional salsa (optional)

1. Cook lasagna noodles according to package directions. Rinse with cool water; drain. Pat dry with paper towels.

2. Spread 2 tablespoons guacamole onto each noodle; top with 2 tablespoons salsa and 2 tablespoons cheese.

3. Roll up noodles jelly-roll style. Cut each roll-up in half to form two equal pieces. Serve immediately with additional salsa, if desired, or cover with plastic wrap and refrigerate up to 3 hours.

Makes 12 servings

Vegetable Nachos

1 cup diced tomato
1 cup corn kernels, slightly cooked
½ cup diced green bell pepper
2 tablespoons sliced green onions
2 tablespoons chopped pitted black olives
2 tablespoons chopped mild green chiles
2 tablespoons white vinegar
¼ teaspoon garlic powder
⅛ teaspoon black pepper
½ (14-ounce) bag corn tortilla chips
1 cup (4 ounces) shredded Cheddar cheese
½ cup chopped fresh parsley

1. Preheat broiler. Mix tomato, corn, green bell pepper, onion, olives, chiles, vinegar, garlic powder and black pepper together in mixing bowl.

2. Spread tortilla chips evenly on baking sheet. Top with vegetable mixture. Sprinkle with cheese. Broil 6 inches from heat 1 minute or until cheese melts. Sprinkle with parsley.

Makes 6 servings

Sweet Pepper Pizza Fingers

2 tablespoons I CAN'T BELIEVE IT'S NOT BUTTER!® Spread
2 large red, green and/or yellow bell peppers, thinly sliced
1 clove garlic, finely chopped
1 envelope LIPTON® RECIPE SECRETS® Onion Soup Mix
1 cup water
1 package (10 ounces) refrigerated pizza crust dough
1½ cups shredded mozzarella cheese (about 6 ounces), divided

1. Preheat oven to 425°F.

2. In 12-inch skillet, melt spread over medium heat; cook peppers and garlic, stirring occasionally, 5 minutes or until peppers are tender. Stir in soup mix blended with water. Bring to a boil over high heat. Reduce heat to low and simmer uncovered, 6 minutes or until liquid is absorbed. Remove from heat; set aside to cool 5 minutes.

3. Meanwhile, on baking sheet sprayed with nonstick cooking spray, roll out pizza dough into 12×8-inch rectangle. Sprinkle 1 cup mozzarella cheese over dough; top with cooked pepper mixture, spreading to edges of dough. Top with remaining ½ cup mozzarella cheese. Bake 10 minutes or until crust is golden brown and topping is bubbly. Remove from oven and let stand 5 minutes. To serve, cut into 4×1-inch strips.   *Makes about 24 appetizers*

Hot & Sweet Deviled Eggs

6 hard-cooked eggs, peeled and cut lengthwise into halves
4 to 5 tablespoons mayonnaise
¼ teaspoon curry powder
¼ teaspoon black pepper
⅛ teaspoon salt
   Dash of paprika
¼ cup dried sweetened cherries or cranberries, finely chopped
1 teaspoon minced fresh chives
   Additional minced fresh chives (optional)

1. Scoop egg yolks into bowl; reserve whites. Mash yolks with mayonnaise until creamy. Stir in curry powder, pepper, salt and paprika; mix well. Stir in cherries and minced chives.

2. Pipe or spoon yolk mixture into egg whites. Garnish with additional chives.   *Makes 12 eggs*

Hard Cooked Eggs: To perfectly hard cook eggs, place them in a single layer in a saucepan. Add enough water to come at least 1 inch above the eggs. Cover and bring to a boil over high heat. Remove the pan from the burner. Let the eggs stand, covered, in the hot water about 15 minutes for large eggs. Immediately run cold water over the eggs or place them in ice water until completely cooled. To remove the shell, crack it by gently tapping all over. Roll the egg between your hands to loosen shell. Peel, starting at large end. Hold the egg under running cold water to help ease off shell.

Hot & Sweet Deviled Eggs

Firecracker Black Bean Dip

1 can (16 ounces) refried black beans
¾ cup prepared salsa
1 poblano pepper *or* 2 jalapeño peppers,* seeded and minced
1 teaspoon chili powder
½ cup crumbled queso fresco**
3 green onions, sliced
   Tortilla chips
   Assorted cut-up vegetables

Hot peppers can sting and irritate the skin, so wear rubber gloves when handling peppers and do not touch your eyes.

**Queso fresco is a mild white Mexican cheese. If unavailable, you may substitute shredded Monterery Jack or Cheddar cheese.*

Slow Cooker Directions

1. Combine beans, salsa, pepper and chili powder in 2-quart slow cooker. Cover; cook on LOW 3 to 4 hours or on HIGH 2 hours.

2. Top with cheese and green onions. Serve warm with tortilla chips and vegetables. *Makes 8 to 10 servings*

Prep Time: 5 minutes
Cook Time: 3 to 4 hours (LOW), 2 hours (HIGH)

Firecracker Black Bean Dip

terrific
lite bites

Cold Asparagus with Lemon-Mustard Dressing

12 fresh asparagus spears
2 tablespoons fat-free mayonnaise
1 tablespoon sweet brown mustard
1 tablespoon fresh lemon juice
1 teaspoon grated lemon peel, divided

1. Steam asparagus until crisp-tender and bright green; immediately drain and rinse under cold water. Cover and refrigerate until chilled.

2. Combine mayonnaise, mustard and lemon juice in small bowl; blend well. Stir in ½ teaspoon lemon peel; set aside.

3. Divide asparagus between 2 plates. Spoon 2 tablespoons dressing over top of each serving; sprinkle each with remaining ¼ teaspoon lemon peel. *Makes 2 servings*

Marinated Artichoke Cheese Toasts

1 jar (8 ounces) marinated artichoke hearts, drained
½ cup (2 ounces) shredded reduced-fat Swiss cheese
⅓ cup finely chopped roasted red peppers
⅓ cup finely chopped celery
1 tablespoon plus 1½ teaspoons reduced-fat mayonnaise
24 melba toast rounds
   Paprika (optional)

1. Preheat broiler. Rinse artichokes under cold running water; drain well. Pat dry with paper towels. Finely chop artichokes; place in medium bowl. Add cheese, peppers, celery and mayonnaise; mix well.

2. Spoon artichoke mixture evenly onto melba toast rounds; place on large nonstick baking sheet or broiler pan. Broil 6 inches from heat 45 seconds or until cheese mixture is bubbly and heated through. Sprinkle with paprika. *Makes 24 toasts*

Crabmeat Crostini

1 pound Florida blue crabmeat or stone crabmeat
1½ cups shredded low-fat mozzarella cheese
½ cup Florida pecan pieces, toasted and chopped
2 Florida datil peppers (or other hot peppers), seeded and chopped
2 teaspoons chopped fresh Florida rosemary leaves
2 teaspoons chopped fresh Florida thyme leaves
1 (3-ounce) package sun-dried tomatoes, rehydrated and chopped
12 (1-inch-thick) slices French bread, sliced diagonally

Remove any shell or cartilage from crabmeat. Combine all ingredients except bread; mix well. Cover and refrigerate for 1 hour. Arrange bread slices on baking sheet and place equal portions of crab mixture on each slice. Broil 4 to 6 inches from source of heat for 6 to 8 minutes or until cheese melts or begins to brown.
Makes 12 servings

Favorite recipe from **Florida Department of Agriculture and Consumer Services, Bureau of Seafood and Aquaculture**

Marinated Artichoke Cheese Toasts

BLT Cukes

3 slices crisp-cooked bacon, crumbled
½ cup finely chopped lettuce
½ cup finely chopped baby spinach
¼ cup finely diced tomato
1 tablespoon plus 1½ teaspoons fat-free mayonnaise
¼ teaspoon black pepper
⅛ teaspoon salt
1 large cucumber
Minced fresh parsley or green onion (optional)

1. Combine bacon, lettuce, spinach, tomato and mayonnaise in medium bowl. Season with salt and pepper; set aside.

2. Peel cucumber. Trim off ends and cut in half lengthwise. Use spoon to scoop out seeds; discard seeds. Divide bacon mixture between cucumber halves, mounding in hollowed areas. Garnish with parsley. Cut into 2-inch pieces. *Makes 8 to 10 pieces*

note

Make these snacks when cucumbers are plentiful and large enough to easily hollow out with a spoon. They can be made up to 12 hours ahead of time and stored covered in the refrigerator.

BLT Cukes

Asian Vegetable Rolls with Soy-Lime Dipping Sauce

¼ cup reduced-sodium soy sauce

2 tablespoons lime juice

1 teaspoon honey

1 clove garlic, crushed

½ teaspoon finely chopped fresh ginger

¼ teaspoon dark sesame oil

⅛ to ¼ teaspoon red pepper flakes

½ cup grated cucumber

⅓ cup grated carrot

¼ cup sliced yellow bell pepper (1 inch long)

2 tablespoons thinly sliced green onion

18 small lettuce leaves or Bibb lettuce leaves from inner part of head

Sesame seeds (optional)

1. Combine soy sauce, lime juice, honey, garlic, ginger, oil and pepper flakes in small bowl. Combine cucumber, carrot, bell pepper and green onion in medium bowl. Stir 1 tablespoon soy sauce mixture into vegetable mixture.

2. Place about 1 tablespoon vegetable mixture on each lettuce leaf. Roll up leaves; top with sesame seeds just before serving. Serve with remaining sauce. *Makes 18 rolls*

Prep Time: 15 minutes

Asian Vegetable Rolls with Soy-Lime Dipping Sauce

Thai-Style Pork Kabobs

⅓ cup reduced-sodium soy sauce
2 tablespoons fresh lime juice
2 tablespoons water
2 teaspoons hot chili oil*
2 cloves garlic, minced
1 teaspoon minced fresh ginger
12 ounces well-trimmed pork tenderloin
1 red or yellow bell pepper, cut into ½-inch pieces
1 red or sweet onion, cut into ½-inch pieces
2 cups hot cooked rice (optional)

If hot chili oil is not available, combine 2 teaspoons vegetable oil and ½ teaspoon red pepper flakes in small microwavable cup. Microwave on HIGH 30 to 45 seconds. Let stand 5 minutes to allow flavor to develop.

1. Combine soy sauce, lime juice, water, chili oil, garlic and ginger in medium bowl. Reserve ⅓ cup mixture for dipping sauce; set aside.

2. Cut pork tenderloin lengthwise in half; cut crosswise into 4-inch-thick slices. Cut slices into ½-inch strips. Add to bowl with soy sauce mixture; toss to coat. Cover; refrigerate at least 30 minutes or up to 2 hours, turning once.

3. Spray grid with nonstick cooking spray. Prepare grill for direct cooking.

4. Remove pork from marinade; discard marinade. Alternately weave pork strips and thread bell pepper and onion chunks onto eight 8- to 10-inch metal skewers.

5. Grill, covered, over medium-hot coals 6 to 8 minutes or until pork is barely pink in center, turning halfway through grilling time. Serve with rice, if desired, and reserved dipping sauce.

Makes 8 kabobs

Thai-Style Pork Kabobs

Baked Egg Rolls

Sesame Dipping Sauce (recipe follows)
1 ounce dried shiitake mushrooms
1 large carrot, shredded
1 can (8 ounces) sliced water chestnuts, drained and minced
3 green onions, minced
3 tablespoons chopped fresh cilantro
Nonstick cooking spray
12 ounces ground chicken
2 tablespoons minced fresh ginger
6 cloves garlic, minced
2 tablespoons reduced-sodium soy sauce
2 teaspoons water
1 teaspoon cornstarch
12 egg roll wrappers
1 tablespoon vegetable oil
1 teaspoon sesame seeds

1. Prepare Sesame Dipping Sauce. Place mushrooms in small bowl. Cover with warm water; let stand 30 minutes. Rinse well. Drain; squeeze out excess water. Cut off and discard stems. Finely chop caps; place in large bowl. Add carrot, water chestnuts, green onions and cilantro; mix well.

2. Spray medium skillet with cooking spray; heat over medium-high heat. Add chicken; cook and stir 2 minutes. Add ginger and garlic; cook and stir 2 minutes or until chicken is cooked through. Add to mushroom mixture. Sprinkle with soy sauce; mix well.

3. Preheat oven to 425°F. Spray baking sheet with cooking spray.

4. Blend water into cornstarch in small bowl. Lay 1 wrapper on work surface. Spoon ⅓ cup filling across center of wrapper to within about ½ inch of sides. Fold bottom of wrapper over filling. Fold in sides. Brush ½-inch strip across top edge with cornstarch mixture; roll up and seal. Place seam side down on baking sheet. Repeat with remaining wrappers. Brush egg rolls with oil. Sprinkle with sesame seeds. Bake 18 minutes or until golden and crisp. Serve with dipping sauce. *Makes 6 servings*

Sesame Dipping Sauce: Combine ¼ cup rice vinegar, 2 teaspoons reduced-sodium soy sauce, 1 teaspoon minced fresh ginger and 1 teaspoon dark sesame oil in small bowl. Makes 5 tablespoons.

Baked Egg Rolls

Shrimp Toast

12 large raw shrimp, peeled and deveined (with tails on)
1 egg
2 tablespoons plus 1½ teaspoons cornstarch
¼ teaspoon salt
   Dash black pepper
3 slices white sandwich bread, each cut into 4 triangles
1 hard-cooked egg yolk, cut into ½-inch pieces
1 slice (1 ounce) cooked ham, cut into ½-inch pieces
1 green onion, finely chopped
   Vegetable oil for frying
   Sliced green onions or Green Onion Curls (recipe page 146, optional)

1. Cut deep slit down back of each shrimp; press gently with fingers to flatten.

2. Beat egg, cornstarch, salt and pepper in large bowl until blended. Add shrimp; toss to coat well.

3. Drain each shrimp and press, cut side down, into each piece of bread. Brush small amount of leftover egg mixture onto each shrimp.

4. Place 1 piece each of egg yolk and ham and scant ¼ teaspoon chopped green onion on top of each shrimp.

5. Heat about 1 inch oil in wok or large skillet over medium-high heat to 375°F. Add three or four bread pieces at a time; cook 1 to 2 minutes, then spoon hot oil over shrimp until cooked through and toast is golden brown. Drain on paper towels. Garnish with green onions. *Makes 12 appetizers*

Shrimp Toast

Green Onion Curls

> **6 to 8 medium green onions with tops**
> **Cold water**
> **10 to 12 ice cubes**

1. Trim bulbs (white part) from onions; reserve for another use, if desired. Trim remaining stems (green part) to 4-inch lengths.

2. Using sharp scissors, cut each section of green stems lengthwise into very thin strips down to beginning of stems, cutting 6 to 8 strips from each stem section.

3. Fill large bowl about half full with cold water. Add green onions and ice cubes. Refrigerate until onions curl, about 1 hour; drain.

Makes 6 to 8 curls

California Rolls

> **1 cup reduced-fat ricotta cheese**
> **2 (10-inch) flour tortillas**
> **1 medium tomato, thinly sliced**
> **2 cups stemmed and torn fresh spinach**
> **1 cup chopped onion**
> **1 cup thinly sliced red or green bell pepper (about 1 medium)**
> **½ teaspoon dried oregano**
> **½ teaspoon dried basil**
> **4 ounces sliced turkey breast**

1. Spread cheese evenly over tortillas to within ¼ inch of edges. Layer tomato, spinach, onion, bell pepper, oregano, basil and turkey over two thirds of each tortilla. Roll up tortillas. Wrap in plastic wrap; refrigerate 1 hour.

2. Cut each rolled tortilla crosswise into 10 slices before serving.

Makes 4 servings

Rice & Artichoke Phyllo Triangles

1 box UNCLE BEN'S® Butter & Herb Fast Cook Recipe Long Grain
   & Wild Rice
1 jar (6½ ounces) marinated quartered artichokes, drained
   and finely chopped
2 tablespoons grated Parmesan cheese
1 tablespoon minced onion or 1 green onion with top, finely chopped
⅓ cup plain yogurt or sour cream
10 sheets frozen phyllo dough, thawed

1. Prepare rice according to package directions. Cool completely.

2. Preheat oven to 375°F. In medium bowl, combine rice, artichokes, Parmesan cheese and onion; mix well. Stir in yogurt until well blended.

3. Place one sheet of phyllo dough on a damp kitchen towel. (Keep remaining dough covered.) Lightly spray dough with nonstick cooking spray. Fold dough in half by bringing short sides of dough together; spray lightly with additional cooking spray.

4. Cut dough into four equal strips, each about 3¼ inches wide. For each appetizer, spoon about 1 tablespoon rice mixture onto dough about 1 inch from end of each strip. Fold 1 corner over filling to make triangle. Continue folding as you would fold a flag to form a triangle that encloses filling. Repeat with remaining dough and filling.

5. Place triangles on greased baking sheets. Spray triangles with nonstick cooking spray. Bake 12 to 15 minutes or until golden brown.

Makes 40 appetizers

Tip: To simplify preparation, the rice mixture can be prepared a day ahead, covered and refrigerated until ready to use. Use a pizza cutter to cut phyllo dough into strips.

Bacon & Cheese Dip

- **2 packages (8 ounces each) reduced-fat cream cheese, softened and cut into cubes**
- **4 cups (16 ounces) shredded reduced-fat sharp Cheddar cheese**
- **1 cup evaporated fat-free (skim) milk**
- **2 tablespoons yellow mustard**
- **1 tablespoon chopped onion**
- **2 teaspoons Worcestershire sauce**
- **½ teaspoon salt**
- **¼ teaspoon hot pepper sauce (optional)**
- **1 pound turkey bacon, crisp-cooked and crumbled**
  Vegetable dippers or crusty bread (optional)

Slow Cooker Directions

1. Combine cream cheese, Cheddar cheese, evaporated milk, mustard, onion, Worcestershire, salt and hot pepper sauce, if desired, in slow cooker. Cover; cook on LOW, stirring occasionally, 1 hour or until cheese melts.

2. Stir in bacon; adjust seasonings as desired. Serve with vegetable dippers or crusty bread, if desired.

Makes 32 servings (about 4 cups dip)

note

Experiment serving different vegetables with this dip. Try raw or steamed asparagus, broccoli, cauliflower, celery, cucumber, green beans, mushrooms, peppers, snowpeas and zucchini. You can enjoy unlimited amounts of these vegetables that fill you up without breaking the calorie bank.

Bacon & Cheese Dip

Savory Zucchini Stix

Olive oil cooking spray
3 tablespoons seasoned dry bread crumbs
2 tablespoons grated Parmesan cheese
1 egg white
1 teaspoon reduced-fat (2%) milk
2 small zucchini (about 4 ounces each), cut lengthwise into quarters
⅓ cup pasta sauce, warmed

1. Preheat oven to 400°F. Spray baking sheet with cooking spray; set aside.

2. Combine bread crumbs and Parmesan cheese in shallow dish. Combine egg white and milk in another shallow dish; beat with fork until well blended.

3. Dip each zucchini wedge first into crumb mixture, then into egg white mixture, letting excess drip back into dish. Roll again in crumb mixture to coat.

4. Place zucchini sticks on prepared baking sheet; coat well with cooking spray. Bake 15 to 18 minutes or until golden brown. Serve with pasta sauce. *Makes 4 servings*

Savory Zucchini Stix

Apricot-Chicken Pot Stickers

2 cups plus 1 tablespoon water, divided
2 boneless skinless chicken breasts (about 8 ounces)
2 cups chopped finely shredded cabbage
½ cup apricot fruit spread
2 green onions, finely chopped
2 teaspoons reduced-sodium soy sauce
½ teaspoon grated fresh ginger
⅛ teaspoon black pepper
30 (3-inch) wonton wrappers
   Prepared sweet and sour sauce (optional)

1. Bring 2 cups water to a boil in medium saucepan. Add chicken. Reduce heat to low; simmer, covered, 10 minutes or until chicken is no longer pink in center. Drain chicken; set aside.

2. Add cabbage and remaining 1 tablespoon water to same saucepan. Cook over high heat 1 to 2 minutes or until water evaporates, stirring occasionally. Remove from heat; cool slightly.

3. Finely chop chicken. Return chicken to saucepan. Add fruit spread, green onions, soy sauce, ginger and pepper; mix well.

4. To assemble pot stickers, remove 3 wonton wrappers at a time from package. Spoon slightly rounded tablespoonful chicken mixture onto center of each wrapper; brush edges of wrapper with water. Bring 4 corners together; press to seal. Repeat with remaining wrappers and filling.

5. Spray steamer with nonstick cooking spray. Assemble steamer with water up to ½ inch below steamer basket. Fill basket with pot stickers, leaving enough space between to prevent sticking. Cover; steam 5 minutes. Transfer pot stickers to serving plate. Serve with sweet and sour sauce, if desired. *Makes 10 servings*

Apricot-Chicken Pot Stickers

*The publisher would like to thank the companies and organizations
listed below for the use of their recipes and photographs
in this publication.*

ACH Food Companies, Inc.

Alouette® Spreadable Cheese, Alouette® Baby Brie®, Alouette®
Crème Spreadable, Chavrie®, Saladena®

Bob Evans®

Cabot® Creamery Cooperative

Campbell Soup Company

Cucina Classica Italiana, Inc.

Dole Food Company, Inc.

Florida Department of Agriculture and Consumer Services,
Bureau of Seafood and Aquaculture

The Hershey Company

Hillshire Farm®

Hormel Foods, LLC

Jennie-O Turkey Store, LLC

©2008 Kraft Foods, KRAFT, KRAFT Hexagon Logo, PHILADELPHIA
AND PHILADELPHIA Logo are registered trademarks
of Kraft Foods Holdings, Inc. All rights reserved.

MASTERFOODS USA

McIlhenny Company (TABASCO® brand Pepper Sauce)

National Onion Association

National Pork Board

Ortega®, A Division of B&G Foods, Inc.

Perdue Farms Incorporated

Reckitt Benckiser Inc.

Sargento® Foods Inc.

Stonyfield Farm®

Unilever

Walnut Marketing Board

conversion chart

VOLUME MEASUREMENTS (dry)

1/8 teaspoon = 0.5 mL
1/4 teaspoon = 1 mL
1/2 teaspoon = 2 mL
3/4 teaspoon = 4 mL
1 teaspoon = 5 mL
1 tablespoon = 15 mL
2 tablespoons = 30 mL
1/4 cup = 60 mL
1/3 cup = 75 mL
1/2 cup = 125 mL
2/3 cup = 150 mL
3/4 cup = 175 mL
1 cup = 250 mL
2 cups = 1 pint = 500 mL
3 cups = 750 mL
4 cups = 1 quart = 1 L

VOLUME MEASUREMENTS (fluid)

1 fluid ounce (2 tablespoons) = 30 mL
4 fluid ounces (1/2 cup) = 125 mL
8 fluid ounces (1 cup) = 250 mL
12 fluid ounces (11/2 cups) = 375 mL
16 fluid ounces (2 cups) = 500 mL

WEIGHTS (mass)

1/2 ounce = 15 g
1 ounce = 30 g
3 ounces = 90 g
4 ounces = 120 g
8 ounces = 225 g
10 ounces = 285 g
12 ounces = 360 g
16 ounces = 1 pound = 450 g

DIMENSIONS

1/16 inch = 2 mm
1/8 inch = 3 mm
1/4 inch = 6 mm
1/2 inch = 1.5 cm
3/4 inch = 2 cm
1 inch = 2.5 cm

OVEN TEMPERATURES

250°F = 120°C
275°F = 140°C
300°F = 150°C
325°F = 160°C
350°F = 180°C
375°F = 190°C
400°F = 200°C
425°F = 220°C
450°F = 230°C

BAKING PAN SIZES

Utensil	Size in Inches/Quarts	Metric Volume	Size in Centimeters
Baking or	8×8×2	2 L	20×20×5
Cake Pan	9×9×2	2.5 L	23×23×5
(square or	12×8×2	3 L	30×20×5
rectangular)	13×9×2	3.5 L	33×23×5
Loaf Pan	8×4×3	1.5 L	20×10×7
	9×5×3	2 L	23×13×7
Round Layer	8×1½	1.2 L	20×4
Cake Pan	9×1½	1.5 L	23×4
Pie Plate	8×1¼	750 mL	20×3
	9×1¼	1 L	23×3
Baking Dish	1 quart	1 L	—
or Casserole	1½ quart	1.5 L	—
	2 quart	2 L	—